D1192909

ENGLISH FOR EVERYONE JUNIOR

BEGINNER'S COURSE

FREE AUDIO
website and app

www.dkefe.com/junior/us

Authors

Thomas Booth worked for 10 years as an English teacher in Poland, Romania, and Russia. He now lives in England, where he works as an editor and English-language materials writer. He has contributed to a number of books in the *English for Everyone* series.

Ben Ffrancon Davies is a freelance writer and translator. He writes textbooks and study guides on a wide range of subjects, including ELT, music, and literature. He also works on general nonfiction books for children and adults. Ben studied Medieval and Modern Languages at the University of Oxford, and has taught English in France and Spain.

Course consultant

Susannah Reed is an experienced author and educational consultant, specializing in Primary ELT materials. She has taught in Spain and the UK and has worked in educational publishing for over 20 years, as both a publisher and a writer of ELT course books for children around the world.

Language consultant

Professor Susan Barduhn is an English-language teacher, teacher trainer, and author who has contributed to numerous publications. She has been President of the International Association of Teachers of English as a Foreign Language and an adviser to the British Council and the US State Department. She is currently a Professor at the School of International Training in Vermont.

ENGLISH FOR EVERYONE JUNIOR

BEGINNER'S COURSE

FREE AUDIO
website and app

www.dkefe.com/junior/us

Penguin Random House

Project Editor Thomas Booth
Senior Art Editor Elaine Hewson
Editors Elizabeth Blakemore, Sarah Edwards, Laura Sandford
Illustrator Dan Crisp
Designers / Illustrators Chrissy Barnard, Amy Child, Shahid Mahmood, Lynne Moulding, Annabel Schick, Kevin Sharpe, Rhys Thomas, Bianca Zambrea
Assistant Art Editor Adhithi Priya
Managing Editor Christine Stroyan
Managing Art Editor Anna Hall
Jacket Designer Surabhi Wadhwa
Jacket Design Development Manager Sophia MTT
Producer, Pre-production Robert Dunn
Senior Producer Jude Crozier
Publisher Andrew Macintyre
Art Director Karen Self
Publishing Director Jonathan Metcalf

First American Edition, 2020
Published in the United States by DK Publishing
1450 Broadway, Suite 801, New York, NY 10018

Copyright © 2020 Dorling Kindersley Limited
DK, a Division of Penguin Random House LLC
20 21 22 23 24 10 9 8 7 6 5 4 3 2 1
001–316826–Apr/2020

All rights reserved.
Without limiting the rights under the copyright reserved above, no part of this publication may be reproduced, stored in or introduced into a retrieval system, or transmitted, in any form, or by any means (electronic, mechanical, photocopying, recording, or otherwise), without the prior written permission of the copyright owner.
Published in Great Britain by Dorling Kindersley Limited

A catalog record for this book is available from the Library of Congress.
ISBN 978-1-4654-9230-2

Printed and bound in China

A WORLD OF IDEAS:
SEE ALL THERE IS TO KNOW

www.dk.com

Contents

About the course 6

1 My friends 10

2 At school 16

3 Our classroom 22

4 My things 28

5 Our favorite animals 38

6 This is my family 48

7 This is my room 58

8 Review: This is me 68

9 At the fair 70

10 Our pets 78

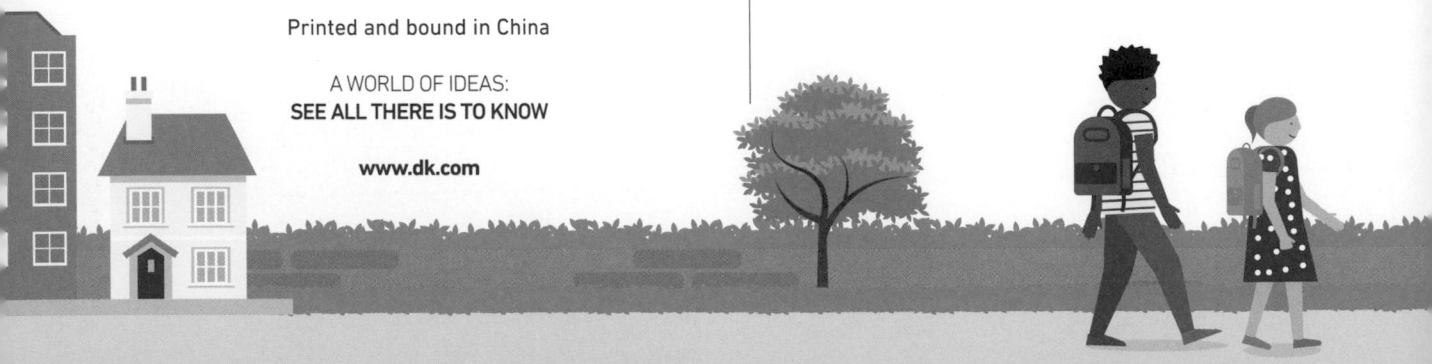

11 My body 88

12 Our town 98

13 My home 108

14 Review: Where I live 118

15 On the farm 120

16 Sports 130

17 At the food market 142

18 At the toy store 152

19 Our hobbies 162

20 Review: What I like 170

21 Our party clothes 172

22 Our day at the beach 182

23 Lunchtime 190

24 At the park 200

25 My day 208

26 Review: Me and my day 220

The alphabet 222

Handwriting guide 223

Grammar guide 228

Answers 234

Grammar index 249

Word list 250

About the course

English for Everyone Junior: Beginner's Course is an entry-level English course for children. The course is divided into 26 units: 22 teaching units and 4 review units. There is audio for all the units.

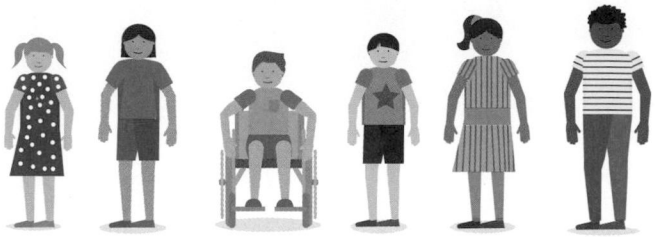

Our characters

A group of six friends—Maria, Sofia, Ben, Andy, Sara, and Max—help present new language in a natural and friendly way.

Unit structure

Each teaching unit starts with a scene that shows new vocabulary, followed by vocabulary exercises. The child then studies and practices three or four grammar rules.

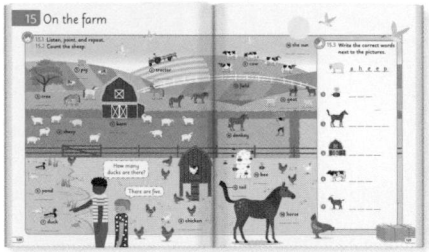

❶ New vocabulary

An illustrated scene presents vocabulary in a clear context. The child listens to and repeats each new word in turn.

❷ Vocabulary practice

All new vocabulary is practiced. The child might be asked to match vocabulary to pictures or spell individual words.

❸ New grammar

Most teaching units contain three grammar rules. The grammar is first explained and then practiced.

❹ New grammar

More grammar is explained and practiced. Many units also have a song to practice new grammar and vocabulary.

❺ New grammar

More grammar is explained and practiced. Throughout the whole unit, new vocabulary is repeated and recycled to help the child.

Audio

English for Everyone Junior: Beginner's Course features extensive supporting audio materials. Listening to and repeating the audio recordings will help the child master the pronunciation and stress patterns of English, as well as help them plant new language in their memory.

Register at **www.dkefe.com/junior/us** to access the audio materials for free. Each file can be played, paused, and repeated as often as you like.

All vocabulary scenes, grammar explanations, songs, and listening exercises have accompanying audio. Clicking on the corresponding number on the app will play the relevant audio file.

Most exercises have accompanying audio. After completing an exercise, the child should listen to the correct answer and then repeat it out loud.

FREE AUDIO
website and app

www.dkefe.com/junior/us

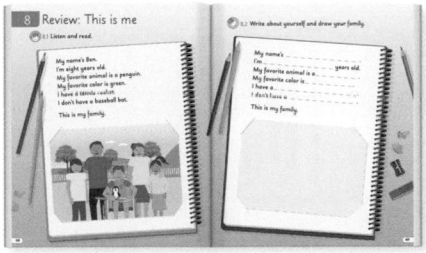

Review units

Four review units provide the child with a chance to read a text incorporating vocabulary and grammar from recent units in the course. The child then writes a personalized answer based on this text.

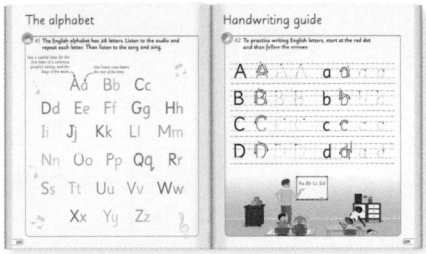

Alphabet and handwriting guide

The course includes a presentation of the English alphabet, together with a guide explaining how to form each letter. The child has space to practice the formation of each letter.

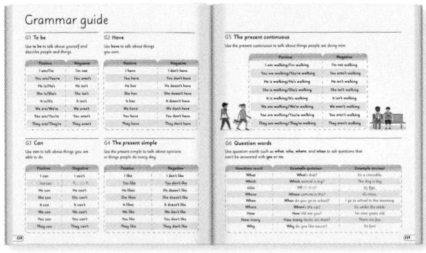

Grammar guide

The key grammar taught in the *English for Everyone Junior: Beginner's Course*, together with common verbs and useful expressions, is presented in a clear and systematic way in the Grammar guide.

Learning new vocabulary

Each unit opens with an illustrated scene showing new vocabulary. The parent or teacher should supervise the child as they listen to the audio on the website or the app and encourage them to point at and repeat each item of vocabulary.

1 First, click on the corresponding unit number (here **Unit 15**) on your screen. Then, click on the exercise number, followed by **Play all**.

2 The child hears the title of the unit, followed by a short dialogue that sets the scene. After this, the audio plays each new word in turn.

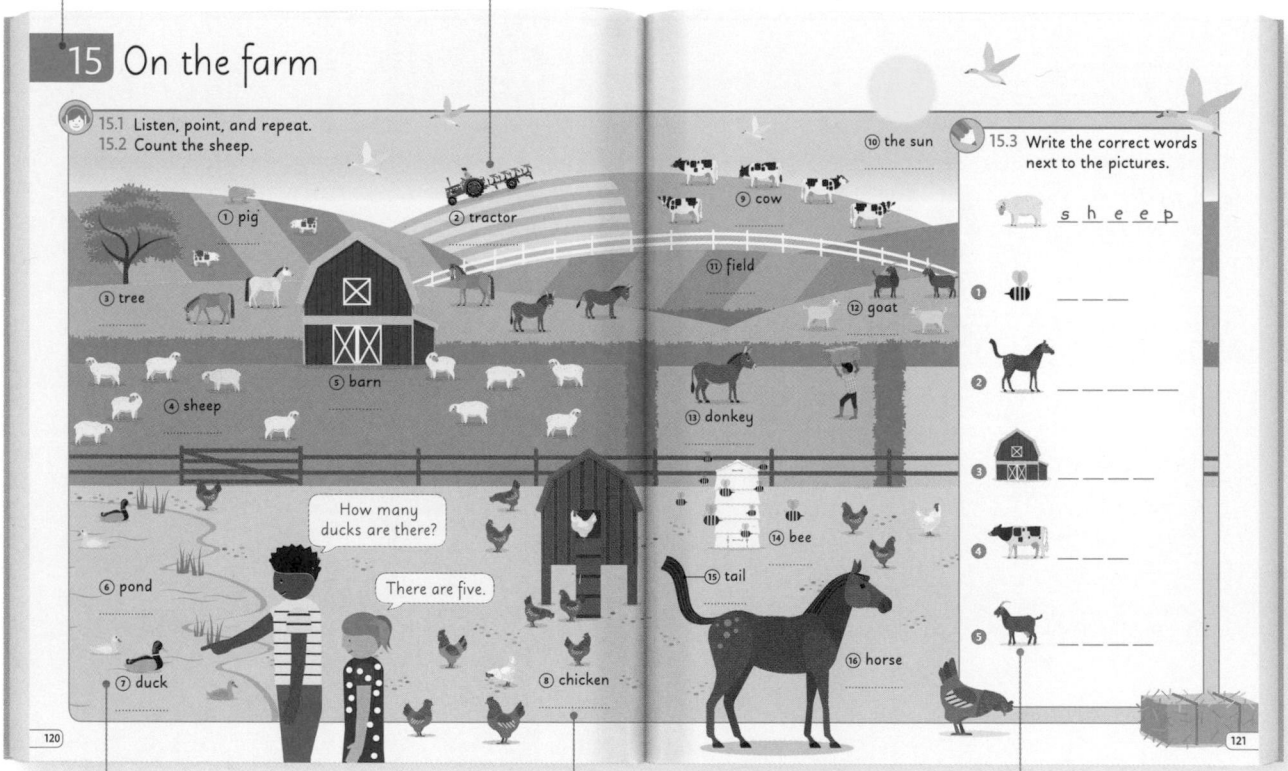

3 The audio stops for a few seconds after each new word. The child should repeat the word during this pause.

4 After listening to the full audio, the child can copy each word on the dotted line beneath it. The word can be listened to again if wished.

5 A short exercise tests some of the new words that the child has just learned.

Learning new grammar

New grammar is explained with the help of a simple dialogue set within an illustrated scene. The child should listen to this dialogue before going on to look more closely at the example sentences together with the teacher or parent.

1 First, click on the corresponding number on your screen (here **15.7**). The child will then hear a short dialogue.

2 Sentences from the dialogue are then broken down into simple parts, with new language in colored or highlighted text. Read through each sentence (and the explanation) with the child.

3 Further information about the grammar for the teacher or parent is included in the **How it works** box.

4 The child then practices the new grammar and vocabulary in an exercise. After this, they can check the answers at the back of the book and listen to (and repeat) an audio recording of each answer.

1 My friends

1.1 Listen to the children.
Hello, I'm Maria. What's your name?
Hello, I'm Ben.
Hi, I'm Max.
Maria
Ben
Max

Hi, I'm Andy. What's your name?
Hi, my name's Sara.
Hello, my name's Sofia.
Andy
Sofia
Sara

1.2 Listen and read.

Hello, what's your name?

Hello, what's your name?

Hello is a greeting.

This is what you say when you ask a person what he or she is named.

To reply, say **I'm**, followed by your name.

I'm Andy.

My name's

Or, instead of **I'm**, you can say **My name's**, followed by your name.

How it works

I'm is short for **I am**. It is the first person singular form of the verb **to be**.
In English, we often use short forms like **I'm** when we are speaking.

I am → I'm
name is → name's

1.3 Listen and match the pictures to the names.

1.4 Listen and read.
Hi, how are you?
Hi, how are you?
I'm fine, thanks.
Hi, how are you?
Hi is also a greeting.
To ask someone how they are feeling, say this.
I'm fine, thanks.
Remember to thank the person for asking.
My name's Sara. What's your name?
And you?
My name's

1.5 Listen, point, and repeat.

1	2	3	4	5
① one	② two	③ three	④ four	⑤ five
.....	.....	.....	.....	.....

6	7	8	9	10
⑥ six	⑦ seven	⑧ eight	⑨ nine	⑩ ten
.....	.....	.....	.....	.....

1.6 Count and write the correct numbers under the pictures.

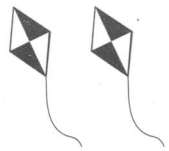

t w o

1 ___ ___ ___ ___ ___

2 ___ ___ ___

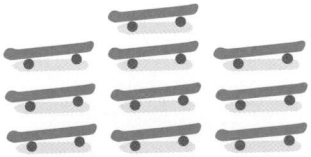

3 ___ ___ ___

4 ___ ___ ___ ___

5 ___ ___ ___ ___

Now listen and repeat.

1.7 Listen and read.

How old are you?

How old are you?

To ask someone his or her age, say this.

I'm | eight | years old.

To tell someone your age, say **I'm**, followed by a number. You can also add **years old** afterward.

How it works

In English, the verb **to be** is used to talk about someone's age. We say **I'm eight**, not **I have eight**.

1.8 Listen and write the correct answers in the spaces.

six | ~~8~~ | seven | 10

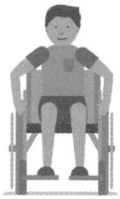

I'm 8 years old.

1 

I'm _____ years old.

2 

I'm _____ years old.

3 

I'm _____ years old.

2 At school

2.1 Listen, point, and repeat.
Sit down, please.
1 playground
2 numbers
12345678910
1+1
3 letters
A
B
C
4 teacher
5 board
6 classmate

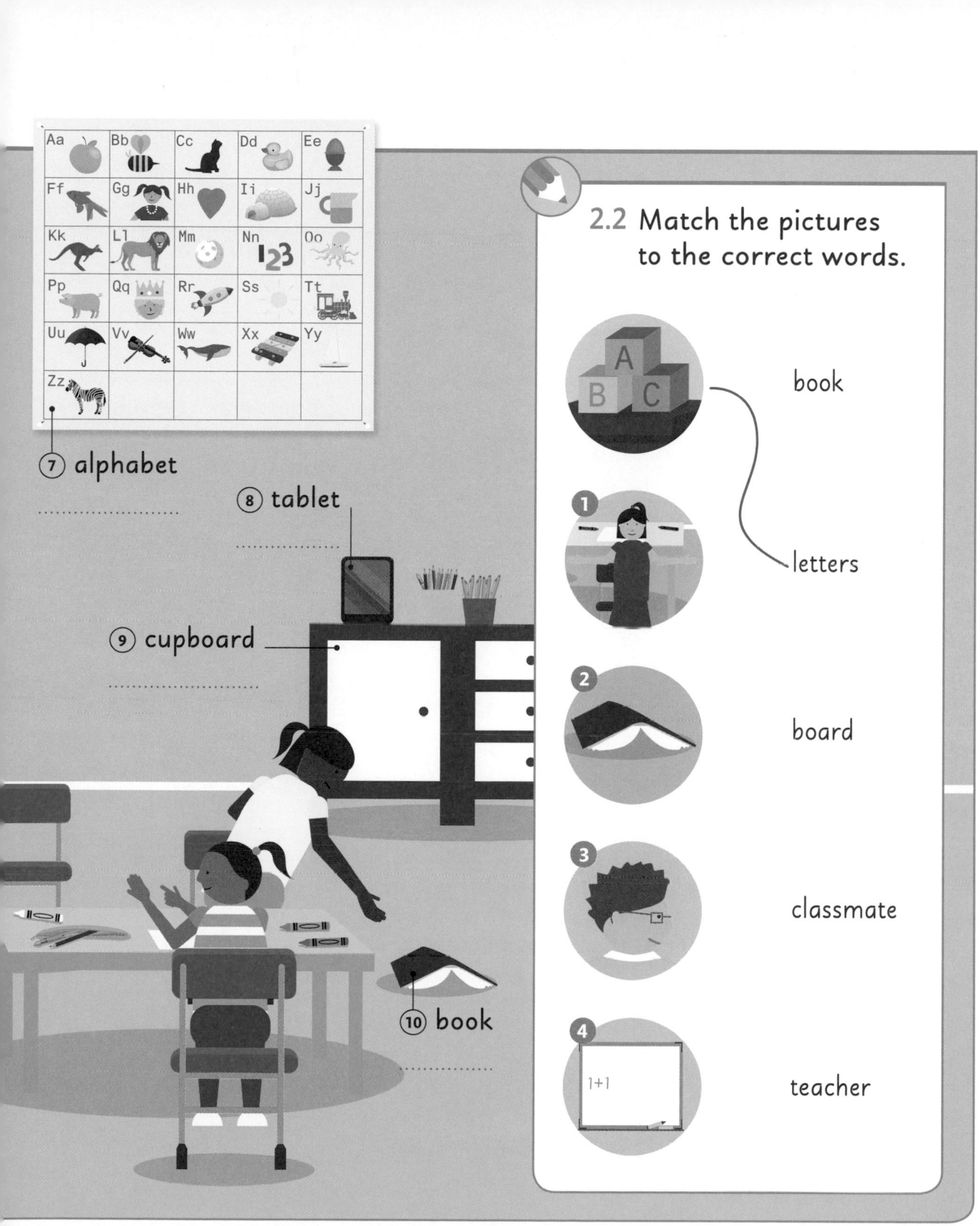
Aa Bb Cc Dd Ee
Ff Gg Hh Ii Jj
Kk Ll Mm Nn Oo
Pp Qq Rr Ss Tt
Uu Vv Ww Xx Yy
Zz
7 alphabet
8 tablet
9 cupboard
10 book
2.2 Match the pictures to the correct words.
A B C
book
letters
1
2
board
3
classmate
4
1+1
teacher

2.3 Listen, point, and repeat.

① look

.....

② find

.....

③ listen

.....

④ show

.....

⑤ add

.....

⑥ open

.....

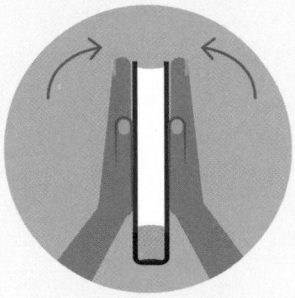

⑦ close

.....

⑧ pick up

.....

⑨ ask

.....

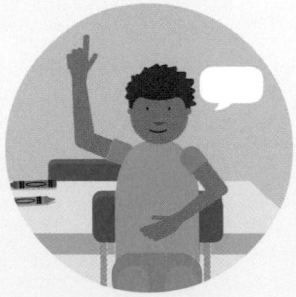

⑩ answer

.....

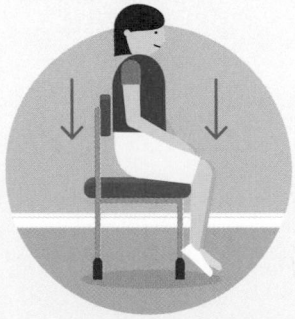

⑪ sit down

.....

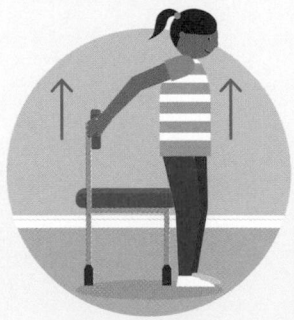

⑫ stand up

.....

2.4 Look at the pictures and circle the correct words.

open / close

1

pick up / listen

2

show / answer

3

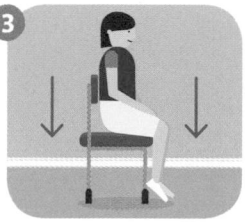

sit down / stand up

4

add / listen

5

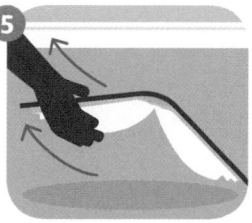

pick up / look

Now listen and repeat.

2.5 Listen and check off the correct pictures.

A ☐

B ☑

1

A ☐

B ☐

2

A ☐

B ☐

3 A ☐

B ☐

4

A ☐

B ☐

5

A ☐

B ☐

2.6 Listen and read.

What's her name?

What's her name?

Say **her** when you ask about a girl or woman's name.

What's his name?

Say **his** when you ask about a boy or man's name.

Her name's Sara.

To reply, say **Her** or **His name's** and then add the person's name.

His name's Max.

How it works

Her and **his** are possessive adjectives. Use **her** to talk about things that belong to a girl or woman. Use **his** to talk about things that belong to a boy or man.

2.7 Look at the pictures and write the correct words in the spaces.

His | her | ~~Her~~ | his

What's her name?

Her name's Sara.

1 What's _____ name?

His name's Dan.

2 What's his name?

_____ name's Hugo.

3 What's _____ name?

Her name's Beth.

Now listen and repeat.

3 Our classroom

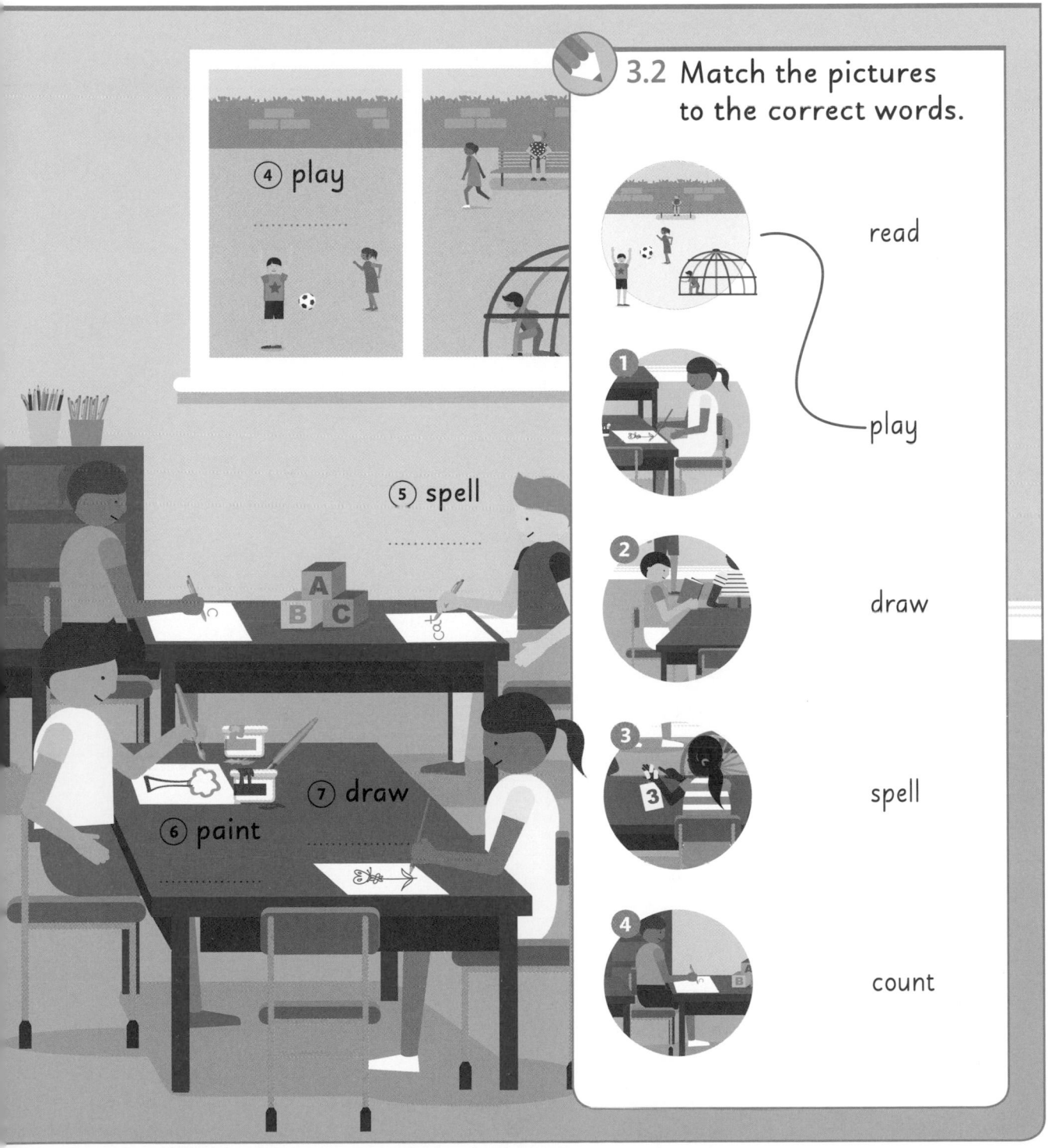
4 play
5 spell
6 paint
7 draw
3.2 Match the pictures to the correct words.
read
play
draw
spell
count

3.3 Listen and read.

Let's paint!

Let's

paint!

play!

Say **Let's**, then add the activity you're suggesting.

How it works

Let's is a way of inviting other people to do something with you. Say **let's**, followed by an activity.

3.4 Listen and sing.

Hello, hello!
What's your name?
How are you?
Let's play a game.

Let's say hello
to my new friends
Max and Maria,
Sara and Ben.

3.5 Look at the pictures and check off the correct sentences.

Let's count! ☐
Let's paint! ☑

Let's play! ☐
Let's count! ☐

Let's read! ☐
Let's write! ☐

Let's draw! ☐
Let's read! ☐

Let's draw! ☐
Let's count! ☐

Let's play! ☐
Let's write! ☐

Now listen and repeat.

3.6 Listen and write the correct words in the spaces.

write ~~play~~ read count

Let's play!

Let's _____!

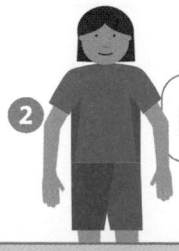

Let's _____!

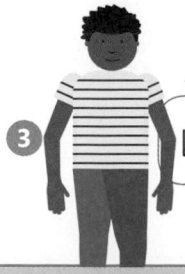

Let's _____!

3.7 Listen, point, and repeat.

11	12	13	14	15
① eleven	② twelve	③ thirteen	④ fourteen	⑤ fifteen
.....	.....	.....	.....	.....
16	**17**	**18**	**19**	**20**
⑥ sixteen	⑦ seventeen	⑧ eighteen	⑨ nineteen	⑩ twenty
.....	.....	.....	.....	.....

3.8 Match the numbers to the correct words.

11	① 15	② 20	③ 18	④ 13
fifteen	twenty	eleven	thirteen	eighteen

Now listen and repeat.

3.9 Listen and read.

One book. Twelve books.

One book.

Twelve books.

Add an **s** to the end of the word when there are two or more things.

How it works

To make the plural for most words in English, add an **s** to the end of the word.

3.10 Look at the pictures and check off the correct answers.

- [x] book
- [ ] books

1

- [ ] pen
- [ ] pens

2

- [ ] teacher
- [ ] teachers

3

- [ ] chair
- [ ] chairs

Now listen and repeat.

4 My things

4.1 Listen, point, and repeat.
4.2 Count the pencils.

4.3 Write the correct words next to the pictures.

r u l e r

1 _ _ _ _ _ _

2 _ _ _ _ _ _

3 _ _ _ _ _ _

4 _ _ _ _ _

5 _ _ _

① pink

.....

② book

.....

③ crayon

.....

④ eraser

.....

⑤ pen

.....

⑥ paper

.....

⑦ ball

.....

⑧ notepad

.....

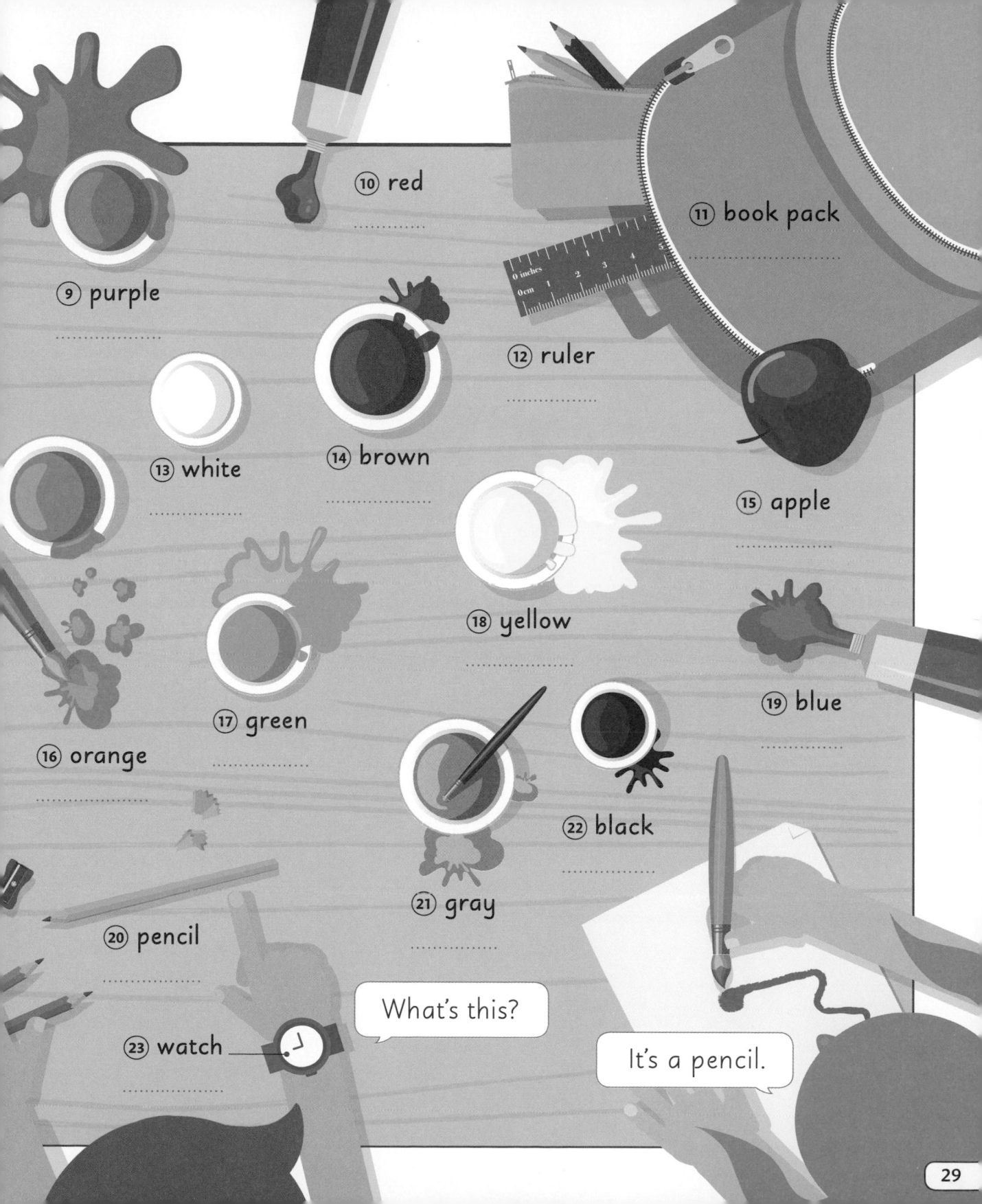
⑨ purple
⑩ red
⑪ book pack
⑫ ruler
⑬ white
⑭ brown
⑮ apple
⑯ orange
⑰ green
⑱ yellow
⑲ blue
⑳ pencil
㉑ gray
㉒ black
㉓ watch
What's this?
It's a pencil.

4.4 Match the colors to the correct words.

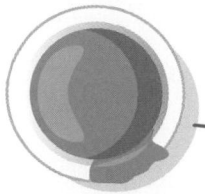

blue

1 orange

2 gray

3 purple

4 brown

5 red

Now listen and repeat.

4.5 Read the words and check off the correct pictures.

pencil A ☐ B ☑

1 book A ☐ B ☐

2 crayon A ☐ B ☐

3 ball A ☐ B ☐

4 notepad A ☐ B ☐

Now listen and repeat.

4.6 There are six words. Mark the beginning and end of each word and write them below.

yellowcrayonwhiteblackgreenapple

yellow

1 _____

2 _____

3 _____

4 _____

5 _____

Now listen and repeat.

4.7 Listen and read.

What's this?

What's **this?**

To ask about one thing, first say **What's**.

To ask about something near you, say **this**.

It's **a** **book.**

Use **It's** to talk about a thing or an animal, but not a person.

It's **an** **apple.**

When the next word begins with **a**, **e**, **i**, **o**, or **u**, put **an** before it.

How it works

Ask **What's this?** when you want somebody to identify a thing that is near you.
When answering, say **It's a**, followed by the thing or animal you're talking about.

What is → **What's**
It is → **It's**

4.8 Look at the pictures and write the correct answers in the spaces.

It's a watch. ~~It's a book.~~ It's an apple. It's an eraser.

It's a book.

1

2

3

Now listen and repeat.

4.9 Listen and read.

What are these?

They're pencils!

What are these?

What are these?

To ask about two or more things, say **What are**.

Use **these** to ask about things that are near you.

They're pencils.

They're pens.

They're crayons.

Use **They're** to describe two or more things.

Remember to add an **s** to talk about two or more of something.

How it works

What are these? is the plural form of **What's this?** Use it to ask about two or more things near you. The answer doesn't need **a** or **an**

They are ➡ They're

4.10 Look at the pictures and write the correct words in the spaces.

crayons ~~pencils~~ rulers
erasers notepads

What are these?
They're pencils.

1 What are these?
They're _____.

2 What are these?
They're _____.

3 What are these?
They're _____.

4 What are these?
They're _____.

Now listen and repeat.

4.11 Listen and sing.

Red,
yellow,
green,
and blue!

Black,
white, and
orange, too!

4.12 Listen and read.

What color is the ball?

The ball is blue.

What color is this?

It's yellow.

What color is the ball?

What color is the ball?

Put **the** before the name of the thing.

What color is this?

You can say **this** instead of the thing's name.

The ball is blue.

Use **is** before the color.

It's yellow.

You can say **It** instead of repeating the thing's name.

How it works

This question uses the definite article **the**. Use **the** when talking about a specific example of a thing.

4.13 Listen and color in the pictures.

1 

2 

3 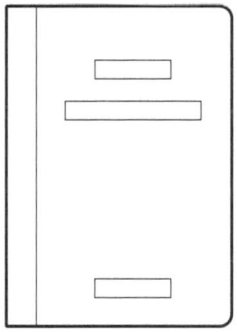

4 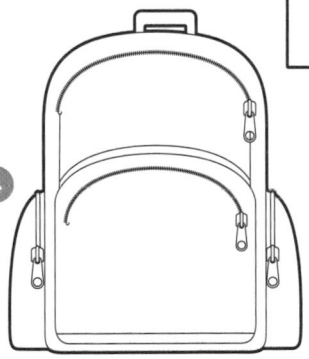

5 

4.14 Look at the pictures and write the correct answers in the spaces.

It's black. It's red. ~~It's pink.~~
It's purple. It's yellow.

What color is the crayon?

It's pink.

1 What color is this?

_____

2 What color is the pen?

_____

3 What color is this?

_____

4 What color is the watch?

_____

Now listen and repeat.

5 Our favorite animals

⑫ polar bear
⑬ bird
⑭ whale
⑮ penguin
⑯ crocodile
⑰ lizard
What's that?
It's a crocodile!
5.3 Write the correct words under the pictures.
l i o n
1
2
3
4
5

5.4 Look at the pictures and check off the correct words.

- snake ☐
- hippo ☑
- crocodile ☐

1

- whale ☐
- parrot ☐
- crocodile ☐

2

- lion ☐
- bear ☐
- monkey ☐

3

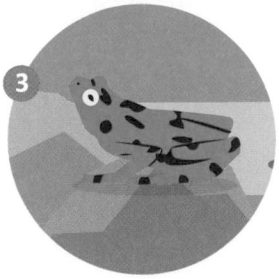

- frog ☐
- tiger ☐
- giraffe ☐

Now listen and repeat.

5.5 Match the pictures to the correct words.

1

2

3

4

snake zebra lion penguin lizard

Now listen and repeat.

5.6 Listen and check off the correct pictures.

A ☐ B ☑

1 A ☐ B ☐

2 A ☐ B ☐

3 A ☐ B ☐

5.7 Listen and sing.

Animals, animals
everywhere!
A lion, a giraffe,
and a polar bear.

A whale and a penguin,
a tiger and a snake,
animals, animals,
they are great!

5.8 Listen and read.

What's that?

It's a lion!

What's that?

What's | that?

Use **that** to ask about a thing that is not near you.

It's a | lion.

lizard.

frog.

How it works

When asking about something near you, say **What's this?** To ask about something that is not near you, say **What's that?** To answer the question, say **It's a** and add the name of the thing.

5.9 Look at the pictures and write the correct words in the spaces.

crocodile ~~lion~~ giraffe bear

What's that?

It's a lion.

1 What's that?

It's a _____.

2 What's that?

It's a _____.

3 What's that?

It's a _____.

Now listen and repeat.

5.10 Listen and read.

What are those?

They're penguins!

What are those?

What are those?

Use **those** to ask about two or more things that are not near you.

They're

birds.

penguins.

polar bears.

Use **They're** to talk about two or more things.

How it works

When asking about two or more things that are not near you, say **What are those?** To answer, say **They're** and add the name of the things. Remember to use the plural form of the thing you are talking about.

5.11 Listen and check off the correct pictures.

A ☐

B ☑

1 A ☐ B ☐

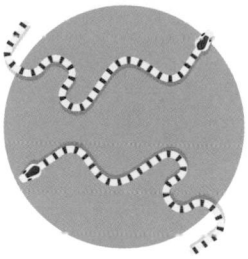

2 A ☐

B ☐

3 A ☐ B ☐

4 A ☐

B ☐

5 A ☐ B ☐

5.12 Listen and read.
What's your favorite animal?
My favorite animal is a tiger!
What's your favorite animal?
What's your favorite animal?
Use this question to ask someone which thing they like best.
My favorite animal is
a tiger.
an elephant.
Remember to use an if the word begins with a, e, i, o, or u.
How it works
You can also use this question to ask about other things, such as a favorite food or color.

5.13 Listen and match the names to the correct animals.

Max ❶ Jill ❷ Grace ❸ Nick ❹ Alice ❺ James

tiger

parrot

snake

zebra

penguin

lizard

6 This is my family

6.1 Listen, point, and repeat.
6.2 Find the giraffes.

① my family

.....

② my grandmother/ grandma

.....

③ my grandfather/ grandpa

.....

④ my father/dad

.....

⑤ my mother/mom

.....

⑥ my brother

.....

⑦ my sister

.....

⑧ me

.....

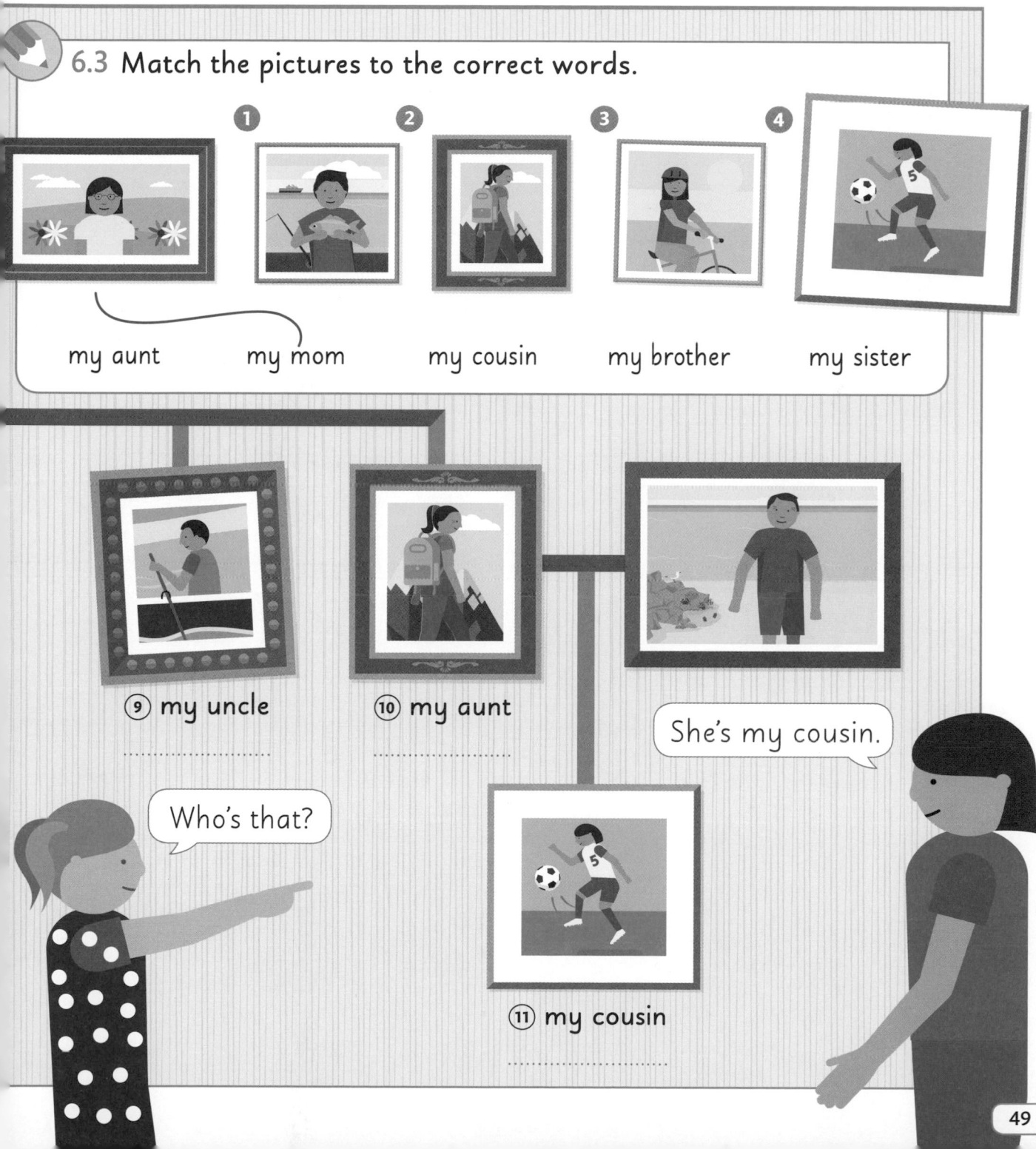
6.3 Match the pictures to the correct words.
1
2
3
4
my aunt
my mom
my cousin
my brother
my sister
⑨ my uncle
⑩ my aunt
⑪ my cousin
Who's that?
She's my cousin.

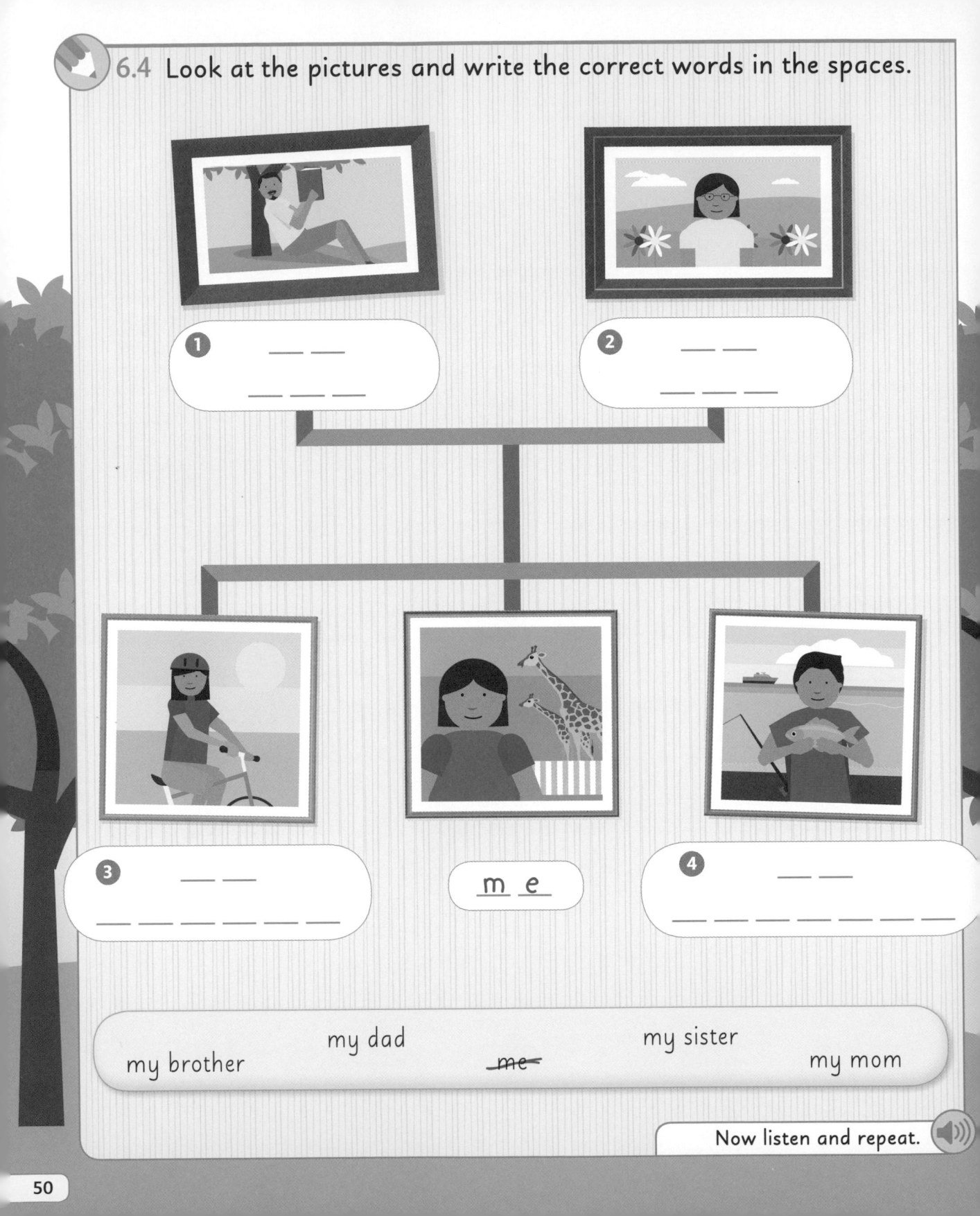

6.4 Look at the pictures and write the correct words in the spaces.

1 ___ ___
___ ___ ___

2 ___ ___
___ ___ ___

3 ___ ___
___ ___ ___ ___ ___ ___

m e

4 ___ ___
___ ___ ___ ___ ___ ___ ___

my brother my dad ~~me~~ my sister my mom

Now listen and repeat.

6.5 Look at the pictures and circle the correct words.

sister / grandfather

mother / uncle

grandma / dad

aunt / brother

mom / grandpa

grandma / father

Now listen and repeat.

6.6 Look at the pictures and write the words in the correct place on the crossword.

6.7 Listen and read.

Who's this? Who's that?

Who's this?

To ask who a person is, use **Who's.**

If the person is near you, use **this**.

Who's that?

If the person is not near you, use **that.**

He's my brother.

To talk about a boy or man, use **He's.**

Use **my** to talk about someone who is related to you.

She's my aunt.

To talk about a girl or woman, use **She's.**

How it works

Who is the question word used to ask about people. **He's** and **She's** are third person singular forms of the verb **to be**. Use **he** to talk about males and **she** to talk about females.

Who is → Who's
He is → He's
She is → She's

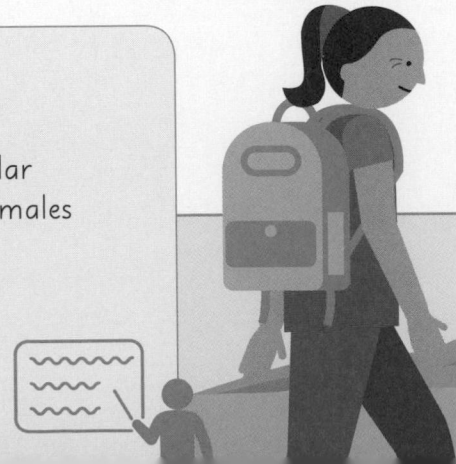

6.8 Look at the pictures and write the correct questions in the spaces.

Who's this? ~~Who's that?~~ Who's this? Who's that?

Who's that?

She's my aunt.

1 _____

She's my mother.

2 _____

He's my grandfather.

3 _____

She's my sister.

Now listen and repeat.

6.9 Listen and read.

Is she your sister?

Is she | **your** | **sister?**

Use **Is she** to ask about a girl or woman.

Use **your** to ask if someone is related to the person you're talking to.

Yes, | **she is.**

You can answer **Yes** or **Yes, she is.**

Is he | **your** | **dad?**

Use **Is he** to ask about a boy or man.

No, | **he isn't.**

You can answer **No** or **No, he isn't.**

How it works

To ask a question using the verb **to be**, put **is** before **he** or **she**.
Your is the possessive adjective to say that something belongs to the person you're talking to.

Is not ➡ **Isn't**

6.10 Look at the pictures and check off the correct answers.

Is she your sister?

- Yes, she is. ☑
- No, she isn't. ☐

1. Is he your uncle?

- Yes, he is. ☐
- No, he isn't. ☐

2. Is she your mom?

- Yes, she is. ☐
- No, she isn't. ☐

3. Is she your cousin?

- Yes, she is. ☐
- No, she isn't. ☐

Now listen and repeat.

6.11 Listen, point, and repeat.

① teacher

② vet

③ farmer

④ doctor

⑤ chef

⑥ police officer

⑦ firefighter

6.12 Listen and read.

She's a teacher.

She's

He's

a teacher.

Use **a** before the person's job.

6.13 Match the pictures to the correct jobs.

He's a vet.

She's a chef.

He's a farmer.

She's a police officer.

She's a firefighter.

She's a doctor.

Now listen and repeat.

6.14 Listen and sing.

Who's this?
She's my mother.
Who's that?
He's my brother.

My dad is a teacher,
my mom is a vet,
Grandpa's a doctor,
and Grandma's a chef!

7 This is my room

13 bed
14 teddy bear
15 baseball bat
16 ball
17 skateboard
18 tennis racket
7.3 Write the correct words next to the pictures.
c h a i r
1
2
3
4
5

7.4 Match the pictures to the correct words.

1 

2 

3 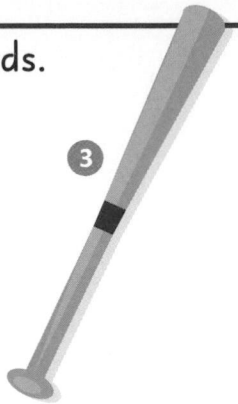

4 

teddy bear camera computer tennis racket baseball bat

Now listen and repeat.

7.5 Look at the pictures and write the correct answers in the spaces.

It's a toy box. They're chairs. ~~It's a ball.~~
It's a skateboard. It's a rug. They're dolls.

What's this?

It's a ball.

1 What are these?

2 What are these?

3 What's this?

4 What's this?

5 What's this?

Now listen and repeat.

7.6 Look at the pictures and write the letters in the correct order.

b d e

b e d

c m r e a a

1 c _ _ _ _ _ _

p e s o r t

2 p _ _ _ _ _ _

c a r i h

3 c _ _ _ _ _

c r a

4 c _ _ _

l p m a

5 l _ _ _ _

Now listen and repeat.

7.7 Listen and read.

This is my toy box.

This is **my toy box.**

Use **This is** to describe a thing that is near you.

These are **my toys.**

Use **These are** to describe two or more things near you.

That's **my doll.**

Use **That's** to describe a thing that is farther away.

Those are **my cars.**

Use **Those are** to describe two or more things that are farther away.

How it works

To talk about one thing that is near you, say **this is**. Use **these are** when there are two or more things.

To talk about a thing that is farther away, say **that's**. Use **those are** if there are two or more things.

That is → That's

7.8 Look at the pictures and check off the correct sentences.

This is my toy box. ☑
These are my toy boxes. ☐

1 

This is my doll. ☐
These are my dolls. ☐

2 

This is my lamp. ☐
These are my lamps. ☐

3 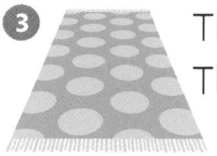

This is my rug. ☐
These are my rugs. ☐

Now listen and repeat.

7.9 Look at the pictures and write the correct words in the spaces.

That's ~~Those are~~ Those are That's

Those are my toys.

1 _____ my poster.

2 _____ my skateboard.

3 _____ my cars.

Now listen and repeat.

7.10 Listen and read.

I have a desk.

I have	a desk.

Say this to talk about things you have.

I don't have	a desk.

Say this to talk about things you don't have.

How it works

To talk about things you own or possess, use **I have** followed by **a** or **an**, then the item.

To talk about things you don't own or possess, use **I don't have**.

Do not ➡ Don't

7.11 Look at the pictures and write the correct names in the spaces.

Sofia

Max

I have a desk.

Sofia

1 I have a ball.

_____

2 I don't have a chair.

_____

3 I have a tennis racket.

_____

4 I have a baseball bat.

_____

5 I don't have a ball.

_____

Now listen and repeat.

7.12 Listen and read.

Do you have a camera?

Do you have | **a camera?**

Say this to ask if someone has something.

Put **a** or **an** before the thing.

Yes, | **I do.**

You can answer **Yes** or **Yes, I do**.

No, | **I don't.**

You can answer **No** or **No, I don't**.

How it works

To ask if someone owns or possesses something, use **Do you have**. You can answer with just **yes** or **no**, but it's better to use a full sentence: **Yes, I do** or **No, I don't**.

7.13 Listen and check off the correct answers.

Do you have a camera?

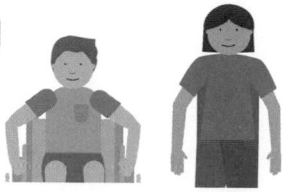

- Yes, I do. ☐
- No, I don't. ☑

1. Do you have a car?

- Yes, I do. ☐
- No, I don't. ☐

2. Do you have a computer?

- Yes, I do. ☐
- No, I don't. ☐

3. Do you have a skateboard?

- Yes, I do. ☐
- No, I don't. ☐

7.14 Listen and sing.

This is my toy box
and these are my toys,
I have a ball
and a skateboard, too.
Toys are fantastic!
Toys are cool!

8 Review: This is me

8.1 Listen and read.

My name's Ben.
I'm eight years old.
My favorite animal is a penguin.
My favorite color is green.
I have a tennis racket.
I don't have a baseball bat.

This is my family.

8.2 Write about yourself and draw your family.

My name's _____.

I'm _____ years old.

My favorite animal is a _____.

My favorite color is _____.

I have a _____.

I don't have a _____.

This is my family.

9 At the fair

9.1 Listen, point, and repeat.
9.2 Find Andy.

9.3 Write the correct words next to the pictures.

h o t

1 ____

2 ____

3 ____

4 ____

① tired

.....

② hungry

.....

They're hungry.

We aren't hungry. We're thirsty.

③ thirsty

.....

4 scared
5 hot
6 cold
7 excited
8 sad
9 happy

9.4 Look at the pictures and check off the correct words.

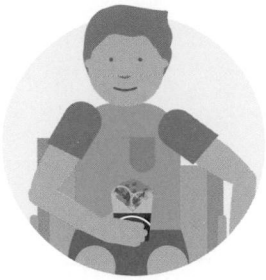

- sad ☐
- hungry ☑
- happy ☐

- tired ☐
- excited ☐
- thirsty ☐

- hot ☐
- happy ☐
- cold ☐

- cold ☐
- scared ☐
- hungry ☐

Now listen and repeat.

9.5 Match the pictures to the correct words.

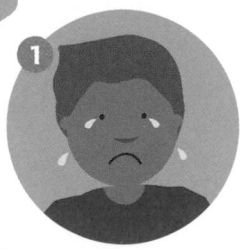

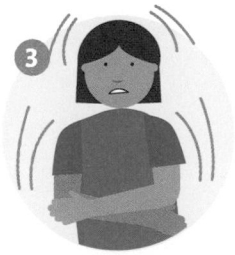

sad excited cold tired happy

Now listen and repeat.

9.6 Look at the pictures and write the letters in the correct order.

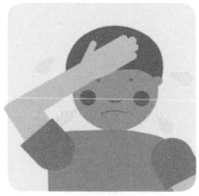

h t o

h o t

1

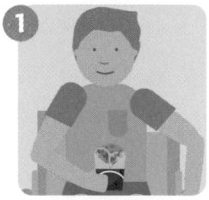

h y g r u n

h _ _ _ _ _

2

h p a y p

h _ _ _ _

3

s d r a e c

s _ _ _ _ _

4

s d a

s _ _

5

t s y h t i r

t _ _ _ _ _ _

Now listen and repeat.

9.7 Listen and sing.

Are you happy?
Yes, we are!
We are at the fair.

Are you tired?
No, we aren't.
We aren't tired
or scared!

9.8 Listen and read.

We're happy!

We're happy!

To talk about a group that you're part of, use **We're**.

They're scared.

To talk about a group that doesn't include yourself or the person you're speaking to, use **They're**.

We're really happy!

They're very scared.

To say how strongly you (or other people) are feeling, put **really** or **very** before the describing word (adjective).

How it works

We're and **they're** are examples of the **present simple** of the verb **to be**.

Put an adjective after the verb **to be** to describe how you (or other people) are feeling. Putting **really** or **very** before the adjective makes it stronger.

We are → We're
They are → They're

9.9 Listen and check off the correct pictures.

A ☐

B ☑

1 A ☐

B ☐

2 A ☐

B ☐

3 A ☐

B ☐

9.10 There are four sentences. Mark the beginning and end of each one and write them below.

We're tired. They're happy. We're hungry. They're excited.

We're tired.

1 _____

2 _____

3 _____

Now listen and repeat.

9.11 Listen and read.

Are you hungry?

Are you | hungry?

Are you can be used to talk to one person or a group of people.

Are they | sad?

To ask about a group that you're not part of, use **Are they**.

Yes, | we are.

To answer on behalf of a group, say **Yes, we are** or **No, we aren't**.

No, | we aren't.

Yes, | they are.

To describe a group you're not part of, say **Yes, they are** or **No, they aren't**.

No, | they aren't.

How it works

Are you and **Are they** are question forms of the verb **to be**.

Are not ➡ **Aren't**

9.12 Look at the pictures and write the correct answers in the spaces.

Yes, they are. No, we aren't. No, they aren't. ~~Yes, we are.~~

Now listen and repeat.

10 Our pets

10.1 Listen, point, and repeat.
10.2 Count the fish.

10.3 Match the pictures to the correct words.

tortoise

1 

spider

2 

dog

3 

cat

4 

rabbit

Look! Andy has a dog.

Yes, it's very dirty.

① rabbit .....

② tortoise .....

③ dog .....

④ mouse .....

⑤ collar .....

10.4 Listen, point, and repeat.
6 spider
7 cat
8 vet
9 fish
1 young
2 old
3 nice
4 scary
5 dirty
6 clean
7 beautiful
8 big
9 small

10.5 Write the correct words under the pictures.

dog cat ~~fish~~ mouse

3 ___ ___ ___

2 ___ ___ ___ ___ ___

Now listen and repeat.

10.6 Look at the pictures and check off the correct words.

☐ clean
☑ dirty

1 

☐ nice
☐ scary

2 

☐ old
☐ young

3 

☐ small
☐ big

4 

☐ beautiful
☐ scary

5 

☐ scary
☐ dirty

Now listen and repeat.

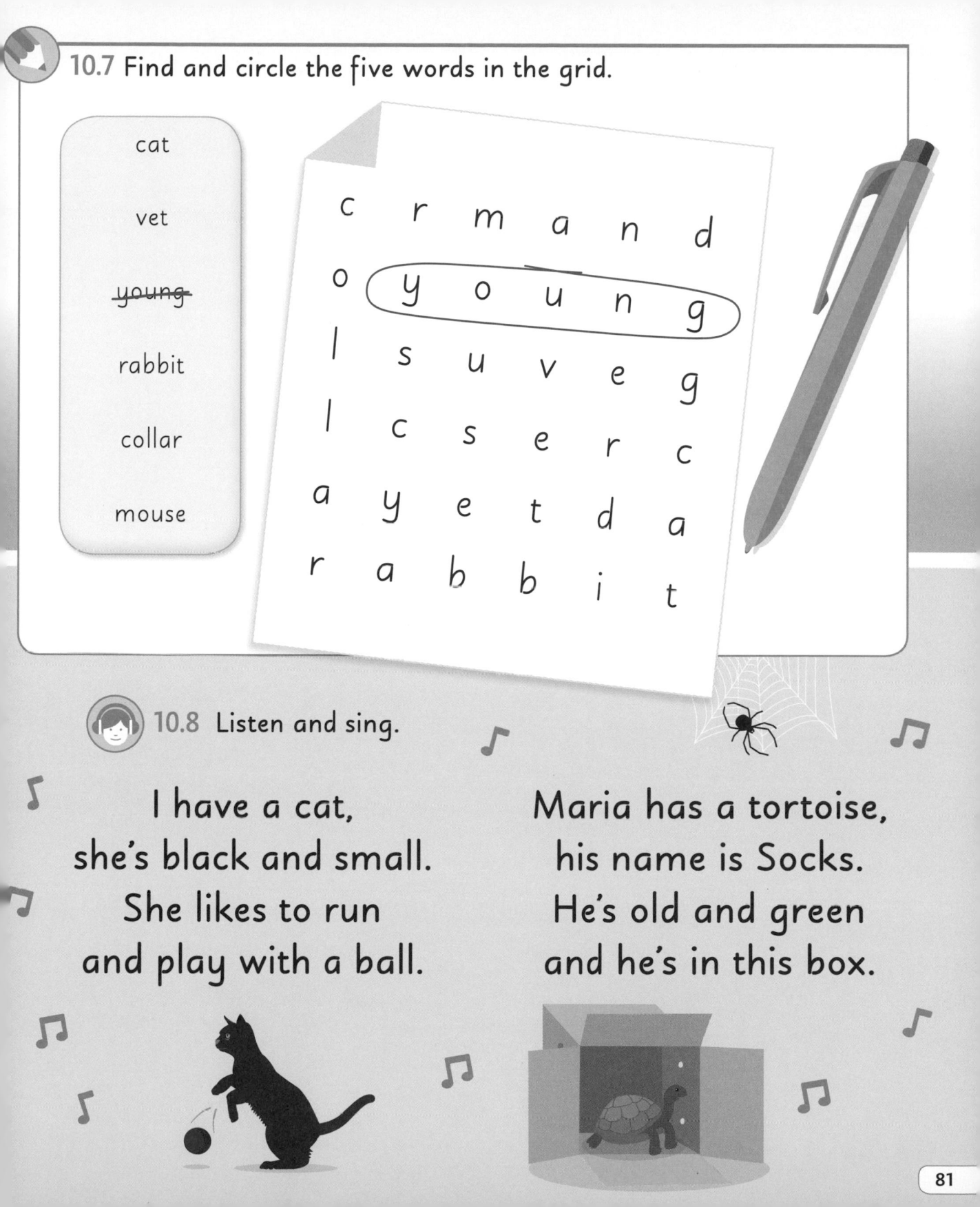

10.7 Find and circle the five words in the grid.

cat
vet
~~young~~
rabbit
collar
mouse

c	r	m	a	n	d
o	y	o	u	n	g
l	s	u	v	e	g
l	c	s	e	r	c
a	y	e	t	d	a
r	a	b	b	i	t

10.8 Listen and sing.

I have a cat,
she's black and small.
She likes to run
and play with a ball.

Maria has a tortoise,
his name is Socks.
He's old and green
and he's in this box.

10.9 Listen and read.

Look!
Ben has a cat!

Sara has a fish!

Ben has a cat.

Ben has a cat.

He has

Use **He has** to say what a boy or man owns or possesses.

Sara has a fish.

You can use the person's name instead of **she** or **he**.

She has

Use **She has** to say what a girl or woman owns or possesses.

How it works

Use **He has** or **She has** to describe what a person owns or possesses. You can also use a person's name instead of **he** or **she**.

10.10 Listen and match the person to the correct pet.

Sara ❶ Dan ❷ Nick ❸ Kate ❹ Anna

tortoise

fish

dog

rabbit

cat

10.11 Look at the pictures and write the correct animals in the spaces.

mouse dog ~~rabbit~~ fish

He has a rabbit.

❶ Ben has a _____.

❷ She has a _____.

❸ Sara has a _____.

Now listen and repeat.

10.12 Listen and read.

Does she have a tortoise?

Does she have | a tortoise

Use these words to ask if a girl or woman has something.

Yes, | she does.

You can say **Yes** or **Yes, she does.**

Does he have | a rabbit?

You can also say the person's name instead of **he** or **she.**

No, | he doesn't.

You can say **No** or **No, he doesn't.**

How it works

To ask if someone owns or possesses something, say **Does she have** or **Does he have**, followed by the thing you're asking about.

Does not → Doesn't

10.13 Look at the pictures and write the correct answers in the spaces.

No, he doesn't. ~~Yes, she does.~~ No, she doesn't. Yes, he does.

Does she have a tortoise?

Yes, she does.

1 Does she have a spider?

2 Does he have a mouse?

3 Does he have a rabbit?

Now listen and repeat.

10.14 Listen and check off the correct pictures.

A ☐

B ☑

1 

A ☐

B ☐

2 A ☐

B ☐

3 A ☐

B ☐

10.15 Listen and read.

Which pet is big?

Which | **pet** | **is big?**

This is the question word.

This is the thing you're asking about.

Which | **one** | **is small?**

You can replace the thing with **one**.

The | **dog.**

Put **The** before the answer.

The | **mouse.**

How it works

To ask a question about a specific thing from a group, use the question word **which.** Put **the** before the answer, unless it's someone's name.

Mouse has an irregular plural form.
mouse ➡ **mice**

10.16 Look at the pictures and write the correct dog's name under the questions.

Ted

Rex

~~Fido~~

Bonzo

Lee

Meg

Which dog is young?

Fido

1 Which dog is big?

2 Which dog is scary?

3 Which dog is small?

4 Which dog is dirty?

5 Which dog is old?

Now listen and repeat.

I have a tortoise.
Do you have a pet?

And you?

11 My body

11.1 Listen, point, and repeat.
11.2 Who has long hair?

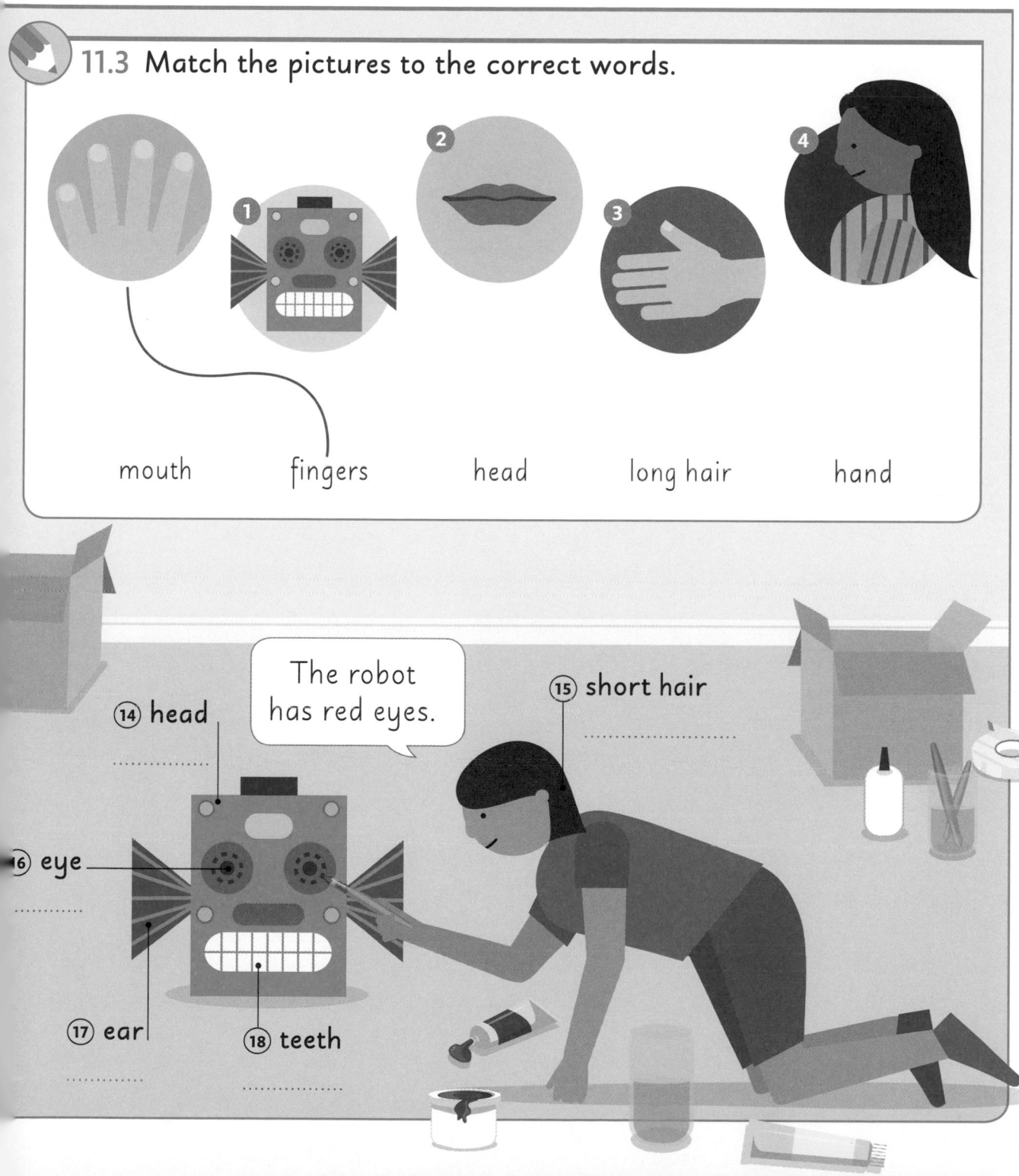
11.3 Match the pictures to the correct words.
1
2
3
4
mouth
fingers
head
long hair
hand
The robot has red eyes.
14 head
15 short hair
16 eye
17 ear
18 teeth

11.4 Look at the pictures and check off the correct words.

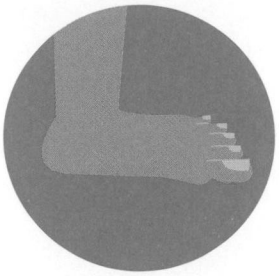

- nose ☐
- foot ☑
- hand ☐

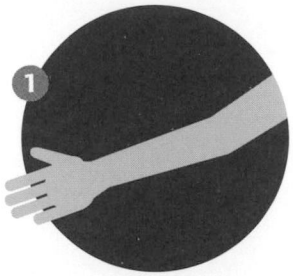

- arm ☐
- head ☐
- leg ☐

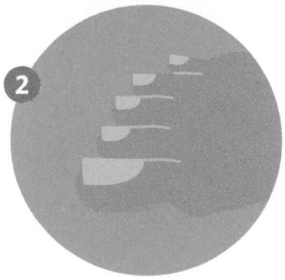

- face ☐
- fingers ☐
- toes ☐

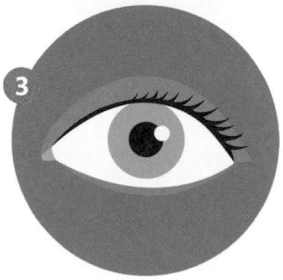

- body ☐
- eye ☐
- mouth ☐

Now listen and repeat.

11.5 Look at the pictures and write the words in the correct place on the crossword.

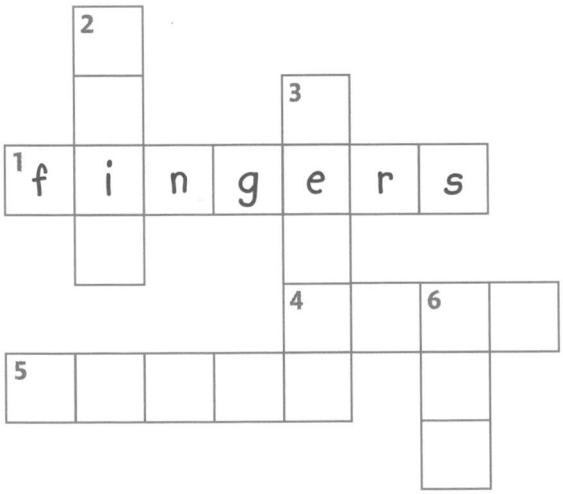

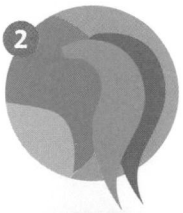

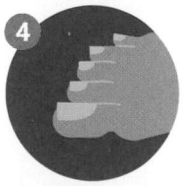

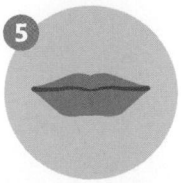

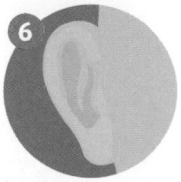

11.6 Look at the pictures and write the letters in the correct order.

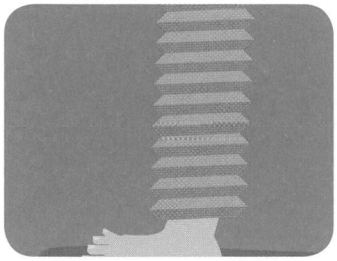

l g e

l e g

h r i a

1 h _ _ _

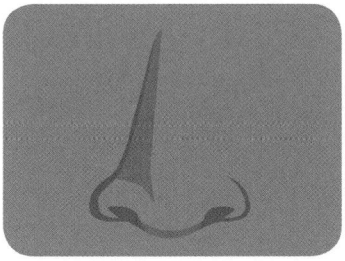

n s e o

2 n _ _ _

f e a c

3 f _ _ _

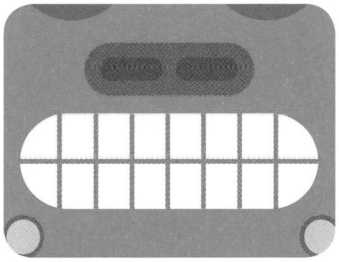

t h e t e

4 t _ _ _ _

b y d o

5 b _ _ _

Now listen and repeat.

11.7 Listen and read.

The robot has red eyes.

The robot has | red eyes.

Say this to describe the features the robot has.

It has | three arms.

You can use **it** instead of **the robot**.

How it works

Use **it** to talk about a thing, an animal, or a place.
It has describes what features an animal, a thing, or a place possesses.

11.8 Listen and check off the correct pictures.

A ☑

B ☐

1 A ☐ B ☐

2 A ☐

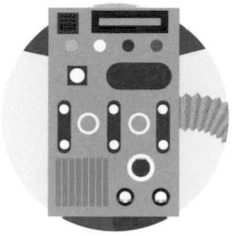

B ☐

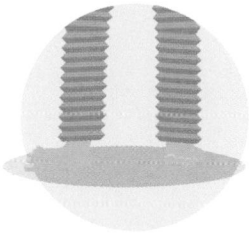

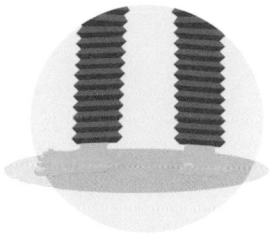

3 A ☐ B ☐

4 A ☐

B ☐

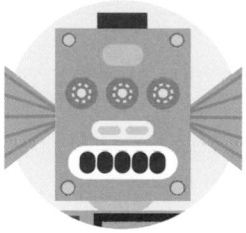

5 A ☐ B ☐

11.9 Listen and read.

Does it have blue arms?

Does it have blue arms?

Say this to ask what features a thing, an animal, or a place has.

Yes, it does.

You can answer **Yes** or **Yes, it does**.

No, it doesn't.

You can answer **No** or **No, it doesn't**.

How it works

To ask if a thing, an animal, or a place possesses something, use **Does it have**, and then the feature you are asking about.

Teeth is an irregular plural.
tooth ➡ **teeth**

11.10 Look at the picture and check off the correct answers.

Does it have green teeth?

- Yes, it does. ☐
- No, it doesn't. ☑

1. Does it have two ears?
   - Yes, it does. ☐
   - No, it doesn't. ☐
2. Does it have purple eyes?
   - Yes, it does. ☐
   - No, it doesn't. ☐
3. Does it have red teeth?
   - Yes, it does. ☐
   - No, it doesn't. ☐
4. Does it have four legs?
   - Yes, it does. ☐
   - No, it doesn't. ☐

Now listen and repeat.

11.11 Listen, point, and repeat.

① touch

.....

② clap

.....

③ point

.....

④ wave

.....

⑤ move

.....

11.12 Look at the pictures and write the correct words in the spaces.

Move | ~~Touch~~ | Point | Wave

Touch your hair!

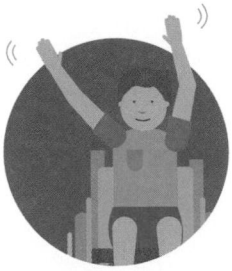

1 _____ your arms!

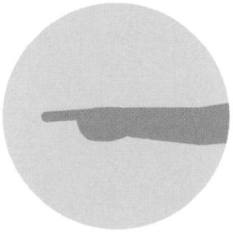

2 _____ one finger!

3 _____ your feet!

Now listen and repeat.

11.13 Listen and sing.

Clap your hands,
touch your nose,
move your feet,
point your toes!

Point one finger,
move your head,
wave your arms,
touch one leg!

12 Our town

12.1 Listen, point, and repeat.
12.2 Count the cars.
12.3 Write the correct words next to the pictures.
b o a t
1
2
3
① airport
② airplane
③ street
④ train
⑤ bike
⑥ zoo
ZOO
⑦ park
⑧ bookstore
BOOKS
Café
Where do you live?
I live next to the fire station.

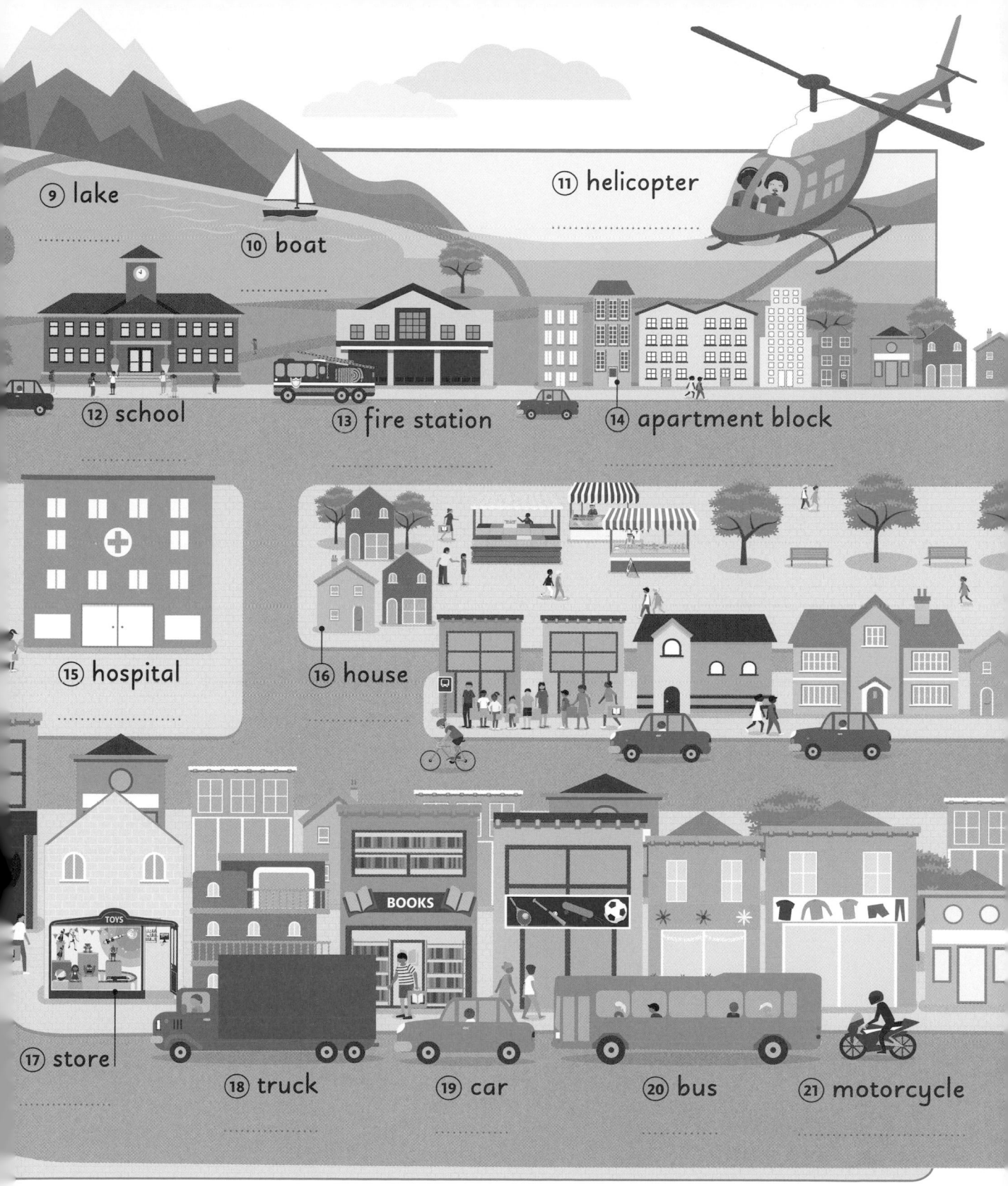
9 lake
10 boat
11 helicopter
12 school
13 fire station
14 apartment block
15 hospital
16 house
BOOKS
TOYS
17 store
18 truck
19 car
20 bus
21 motorcycle

12.4 Look at the pictures and write the words in the correct place on the crossword.

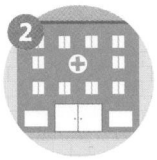

12.5 Match the pictures to the correct words.

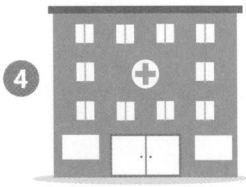

fire station motorcycle hospital bus airplane

Now listen and repeat.

12.6 Find and circle the five words in the grid.

zoo

bus

~~train~~

street

lake

school

s	t	r	e	e	t
c	l	p	o	b	n
h	t	r	a	i	n
o	b	u	s	k	r
o	l	a	k	e	e
l	z	k	z	o	o

12.7 Listen and sing.

This is my town,
there's a park and a zoo.
There's an airport, a lake,
and a fire station, too.

This is my town,
there are cars and a school.
This is my town,
I love it, it's cool.

12.8 Listen and read.

There's a park.

There's a park.

Use **There's** to say that something is present.

There are two bookstores.

Use **There are** to talk about two or more things.

How it works

To say that a thing is present, say **There's**, followed by **a** and the name of the thing you're talking about. To talk about two or more things, say **There are**, followed by a number and the plural form.

12.9 Look at the pictures and circle the correct words.

There's / There are a park.

1 There's / There are two trucks.

2 There's / There are a school.

3 There's / There are a zoo.

4 There's / There are four cars.

5 There's / There are three boats.

Now listen and repeat.

12.10 Listen, point, and repeat.

① in front of

.....

② behind

.....

③ between

.....

④ next to

.....

12.11 Listen and read.

Where's my bike?

Where's my bike?

Where is the question word to ask where something is.

It's behind the store.

Prepositions, such as **behind**, say where something is.

How it works

To ask about a thing's location, say **Where's**, followed by the thing. To describe where it is, say **It's**, then add a preposition and the location.
Prepositions, such as **next to** or **behind**, describe the location of something.

Where is → Where's

12.12 Look at the pictures and write the correct words in the spaces.

between ~~in front of~~ next to behind in front of

Where's my bike?

It's **in front of** the store.

1 Where's your house?

It's _____ the store.

2 Where's the bus?

It's _____ the hospital.

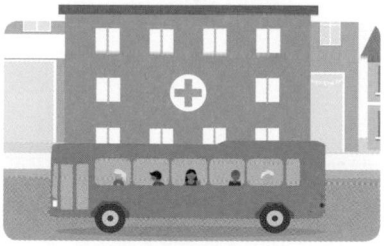

3 Where's the fire station?

It's _____ the school.

4 Where's the apartment block?

It's _____ the park and the store.

Now listen and repeat.

12.13 Listen and read.

Where do you live?

Where do you live?

Say this to ask someone where their home is.

I live **next to** **the school.**

Say this to talk about where your home is.

Use a preposition to be more specific.

How it works

Use the verb **to live** to talk about where your home is.

12.14 Listen and check off the correct pictures.

A ☑

B ☐

1 A ☐

B ☐

2 A ☐

B ☐

3 A ☐

B ☐

13 My home

13.1 Listen, point, and repeat.
13.2 Which room is next to the dining room?
13.3 Match the pictures to the correct words.
1
2
3
kitchen
dining room
bedroom
bathroom
① garden
② bedroom
③ clock
④ plants
⑬ living room
⑭ television/TV
⑮ couch
Where's Sara?
She's in the bedroom.

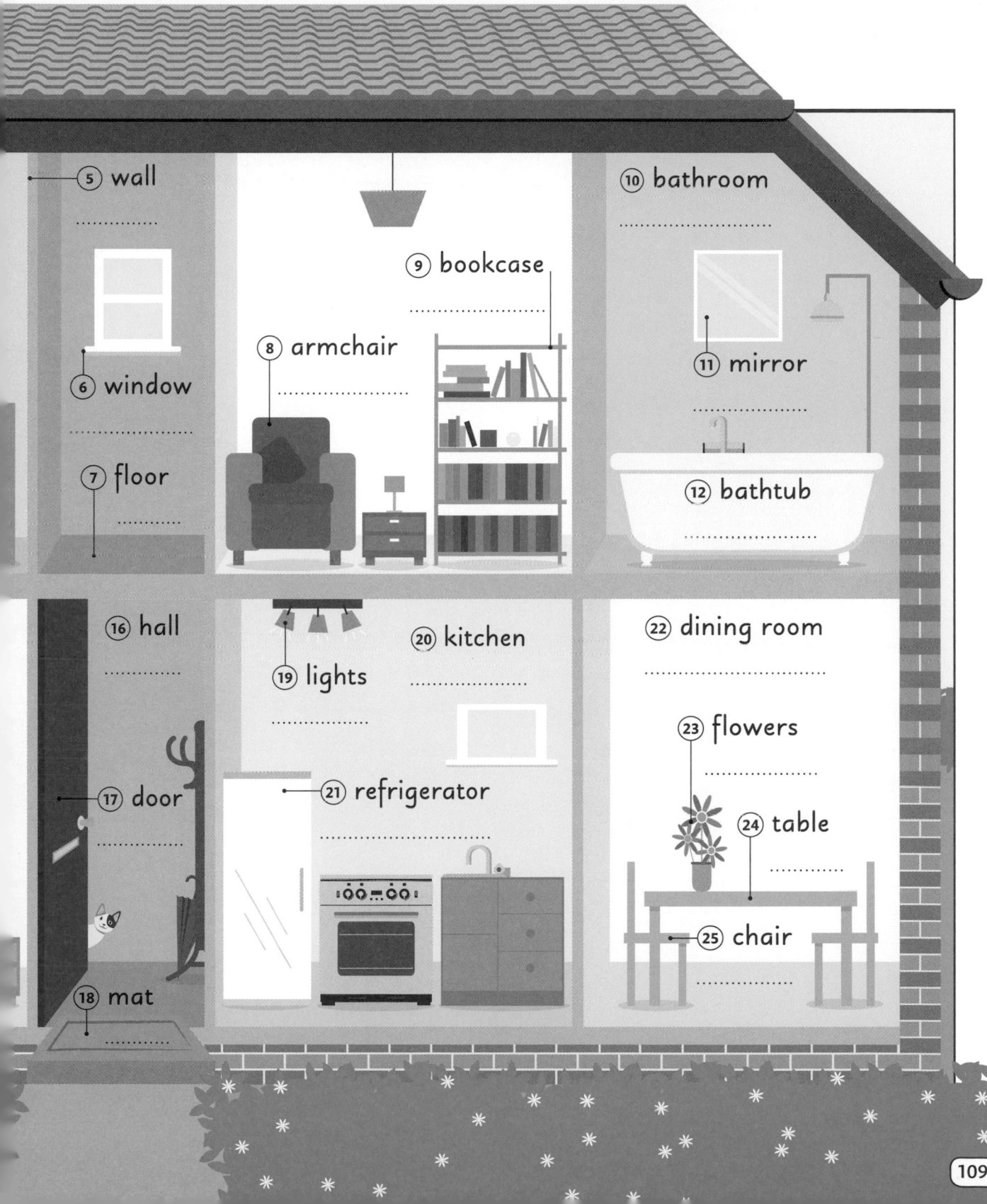
5 wall
6 window
7 floor
8 armchair
9 bookcase
10 bathroom
11 mirror
12 bathtub
16 hall
17 door
18 mat
19 lights
20 kitchen
21 refrigerator
22 dining room
23 flowers
24 table
25 chair

13.4 Look at the pictures and write the correct answers in the spaces.

It's a television. ~~It's an armchair.~~ It's a refrigerator.
It's a door. It's a bookcase. It's a couch.

What's this?

It's an armchair.

1 What's this?

2 What's this?

3 What's this?

4 What's this?

5 What's this?

Now listen and repeat.

13.5 Look at the pictures and write the words in the correct place on the crossword.

1

2

3

4

5

6

13.6 Look at the pictures and write the letters in the correct order.

t b e l a

t a b l e

h l l a

1 h _ _ _

p t l a n s

2 p _ _ _ _ _

w n i w o d

3 w _ _ _ _ _

l g t s h i

4 l _ _ _ _ _

w l a l

5 w _ _ _

Now listen and repeat.

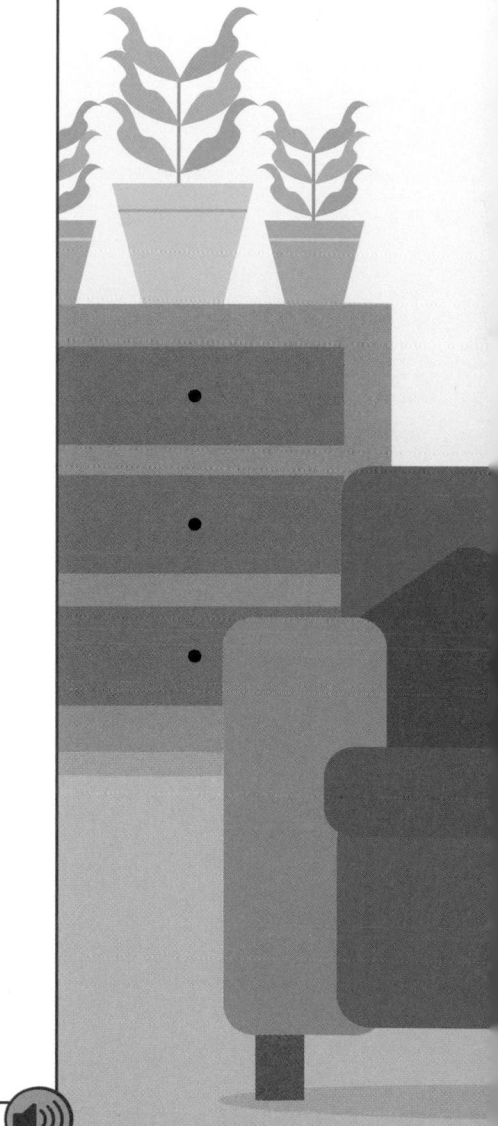

13.7 Listen, point, and repeat.

① in

.....

② on

.....

③ under

.....

13.8 Listen and read.

Where's the cat?

It's under the table!

Where's the cat?

Where's the cat?

It's under the table.

This word describes where the cat is.

How it works

Use **Where's** to ask about someone or something's location. Prepositions, like **in**, **on**, and **under**, describe the thing or person's location.

Where is → Where's

13.9 Listen and check off the correct pictures.

A ☐

B ☑

1 A ☐

B ☐

2 A ☐

B ☐

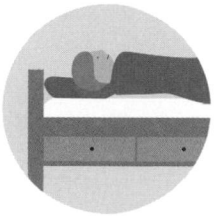

3 A ☐

B ☐

13.10 Listen and sing.

The TV's in
the living room,
the mat is in the hall.

Where's the clock?
It's on my
bedroom wall.

13.11 Listen and read.

Is there a TV in the living room?

Is there | **a TV** | **in the living room?**

Use these words to ask if something is present.

Then add the thing you're asking about.

You can also mention a specific place.

Yes, | **there is.**

You can answer **Yes** or **Yes, there is.**

No, | **there isn't.**

You can answer **No** or **No, there isn't.**

How it works

Use **Is there** to ask if something is located somewhere. Put **a** or **an** before the thing you're asking about.

13.12 Look at the picture and write the correct answers in the spaces.

Yes, there is. No, there isn't. ~~Yes, there is.~~
No, there isn't. Yes, there is. No, there isn't.

Is there a TV in the living room?
Yes, there is.

1. Is there a table in the kitchen?
_____

2. Is there a clock in the kitchen?
_____

3. Is there a bathtub in the bathroom?
_____

4. Is there a couch in the living room?
_____

5. Is there a bookcase in the bedroom?
_____

Now listen and repeat.

13.13 Listen and read.

Are there any flowers in the dining room?

Are there any | **flowers** | **in the dining room?**

Use these words to ask about two or more things.

We use **any** after **Are there**.

Yes, | **there are.**

If the things are present, say **Yes** or **Yes, there are.**

No, | **there aren't.**

If the things aren't present, say **No** or **No, there aren't.**

How it works

Use **Are there** to ask if two or more things are located somewhere. When asking about two or more things, instead of **a** or **an**, use **any**, followed by the plural form of the thing you're asking about.

13.14 Look at the pictures and check off the correct answers.

Are there any clocks?

Yes, there are. ☐

No, there aren't. ☑

1 Are there any plants?

Yes, there are. ☐

No, there aren't. ☐

2 Are there any chairs?

Yes, there are. ☐

No, there aren't. ☐

3 Are there any windows?

Yes, there are. ☐

No, there aren't. ☐

4 Are there any beds?

Yes, there are. ☐

No, there aren't. ☐

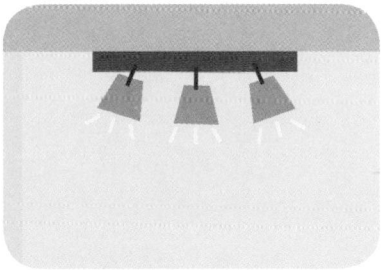

5 Are there any lights?

Yes, there are. ☐

No, there aren't. ☐

Now listen and repeat.

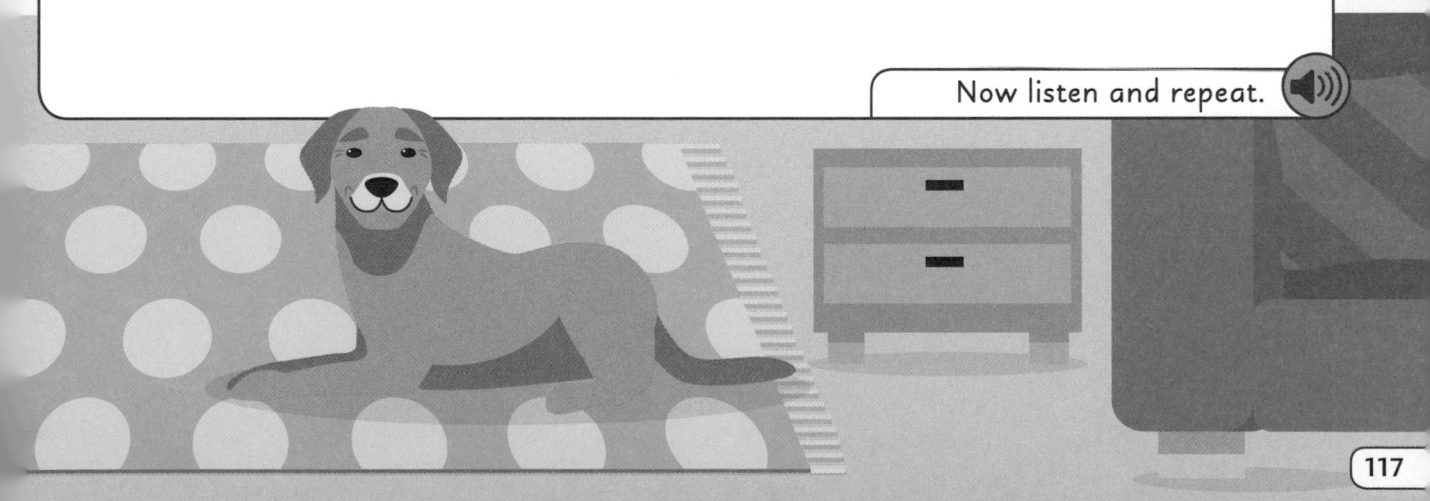

14 Review: Where I live

14.1 Listen and read.

I'm Maria and this is my home. I live next to a park.

In my home, there's a dining room and a kitchen. There are two bedrooms. That is my bedroom. There's a clock and a toy box in my bedroom. My favorite toy is my teddy bear.

14.2 Write about your home and draw your bedroom.

I'm _____ and this is my home.
I live _____.

In my home, there's a _____ and a _____. There are _____.
That is my bedroom. There's a _____ and a _____ in my bedroom.
My favorite toy is my _____.

15 On the farm

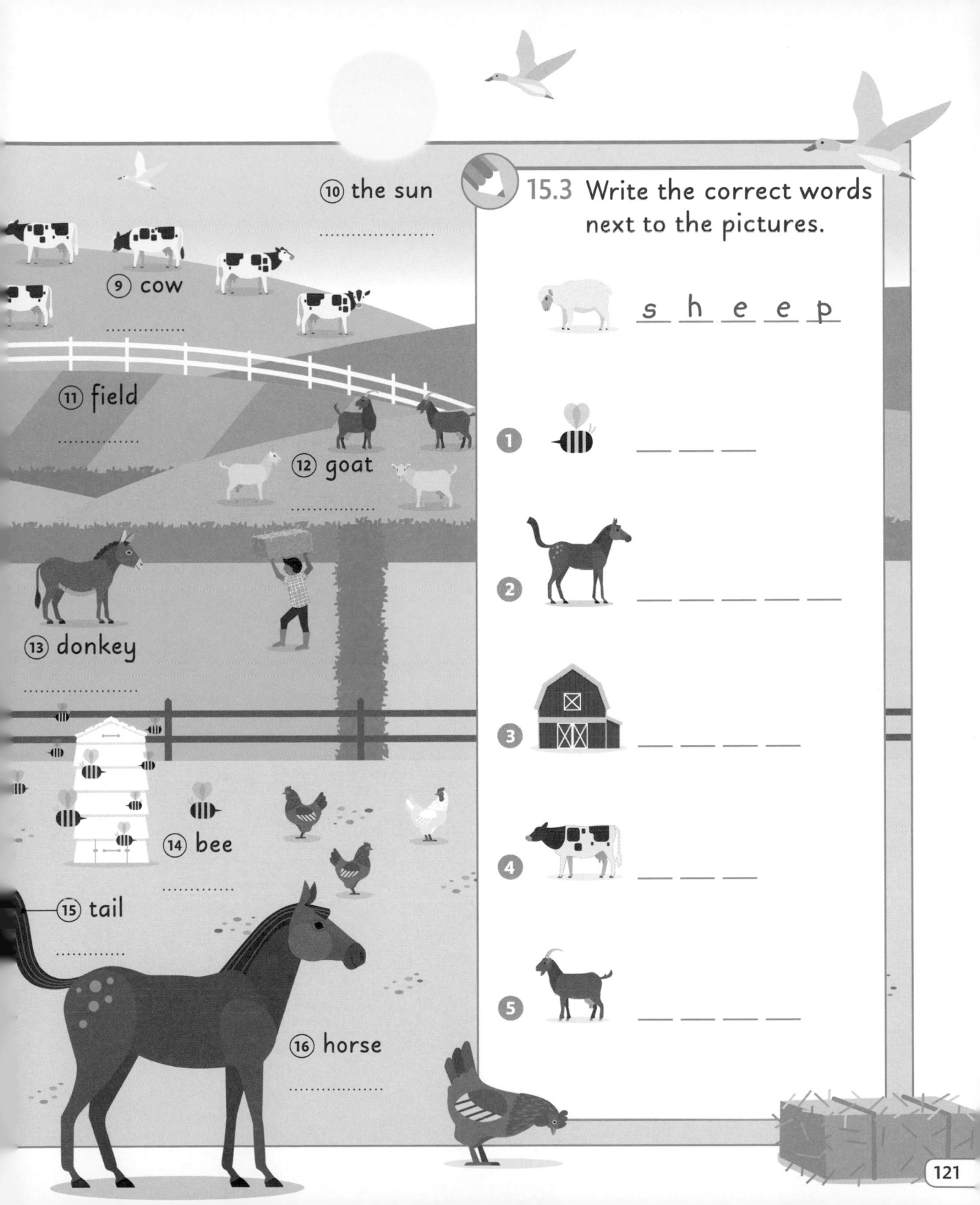
⑩ the sun
⑨ cow
⑪ field
⑫ goat
⑬ donkey
⑭ bee
⑮ tail
⑯ horse
15.3 Write the correct words next to the pictures.
s h e e p
1
2
3
4
5

15.4 Match the pictures to the correct words.

tractor

1 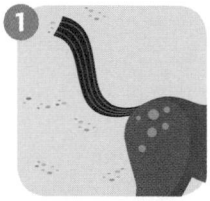

chicken

2 

barn

3 

tail

4 

donkey

5 

the sun

Now listen and repeat.

15.5 Look at the pictures and write the letters in the correct order.

s p e h e

s h e e p

1 

g t o a

g ___ ___ ___

2 

h e r s o

h ___ ___ ___ ___

3 

d k c u

d ___ ___ ___

4 

t e r e

t ___ ___ ___

Now listen and repeat.

15.6 Look at the pictures and write the words in the correct place on the crossword.

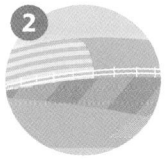

15.7 Listen and read.

How many horses are there?

How many | horses | are there?

To ask about the number of people, animals, or things, say **How many**.

Add **are there** at the end of the question.

There are | two.

Say this when there are two or more.

There's | one.

Say this when there's only one.

How it works

Use **How many** to ask about the number of people, animals, or things there are. Add the plural form of the thing you're asking about, followed by **are there**.

15.8 Look at the pictures and write the correct answers in the spaces.

There's one. There are four. ~~There are two.~~ There are three.

How many horses are there?

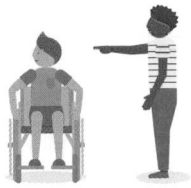

There are two.

1 How many ducks are there?

_____

2 How many goats are there?

_____

3 How many donkeys are there?

_____

Now listen and repeat.

15.9 Listen and read.

Where are the ducks?

Where | **are** | **the ducks?**

Say **are** when you ask about two or more things.

They're | **in** | **the pond.**

To answer the question, begin with **They're**.

Then add a preposition, such as **in** or **on**, followed by the place.

How it works

To ask about the location of two or more things, say **Where are**, then add the thing you are asking about in its plural form. We often put **the** before the noun.

15.10 Listen and match the questions to the correct answers.

Where are the ducks?	They're in front of the barn.
1 Where are the horses?	They're in the field.
2 Where are the chickens?	They're in the barn.
3 Where are the goats?	They're in the pond.
4 Where are the donkeys?	They're next to the pond.
5 Where are the pigs?	They're under the tree.

15.11 Listen and sing.

Where are the ducks?
They're in the pond!

Where are the goats?
They're in the field!

Where are the cows?
They're in the barn!

Where are the animals?
They're on my farm!

15.12 Listen and read.

The goat's next to the tree.

The goat's | **next to** | **the tree.**

Say the name, animal, or thing, followed by **is** or **'s**.

Add a preposition, such as **next to** or **under**, and then the place.

The cows | **are** | **in** | **the field.**

If you are talking about two or more of something, use **are**.

How it works

To describe where something is, first say the name of the thing, followed by **is**, **'s**, or **are**. Then add a preposition, followed by the place.

The goat is ➡ The goat's

15.13 Read the story. Then look at the picture and write the correct words in the spaces.

This is my farm. My cow ___is___ under the tree.

There ❶ _____ four ducks ❷ _____ the pond.

The three chickens ❸ _____ next to the horse.

The donkey ❹ _____ in the field, and five sheep

❺ _____ in front of the barn.

are | is | ~~is~~ | are | in | are

Now listen and repeat.

16 Sports

16.1 Listen, point, and repeat.
16.2 Where is Sara?
1 basketball
2 baseball
3 soccer
4 tennis
Can you play tennis?
No, I can't, but I can play badminton.

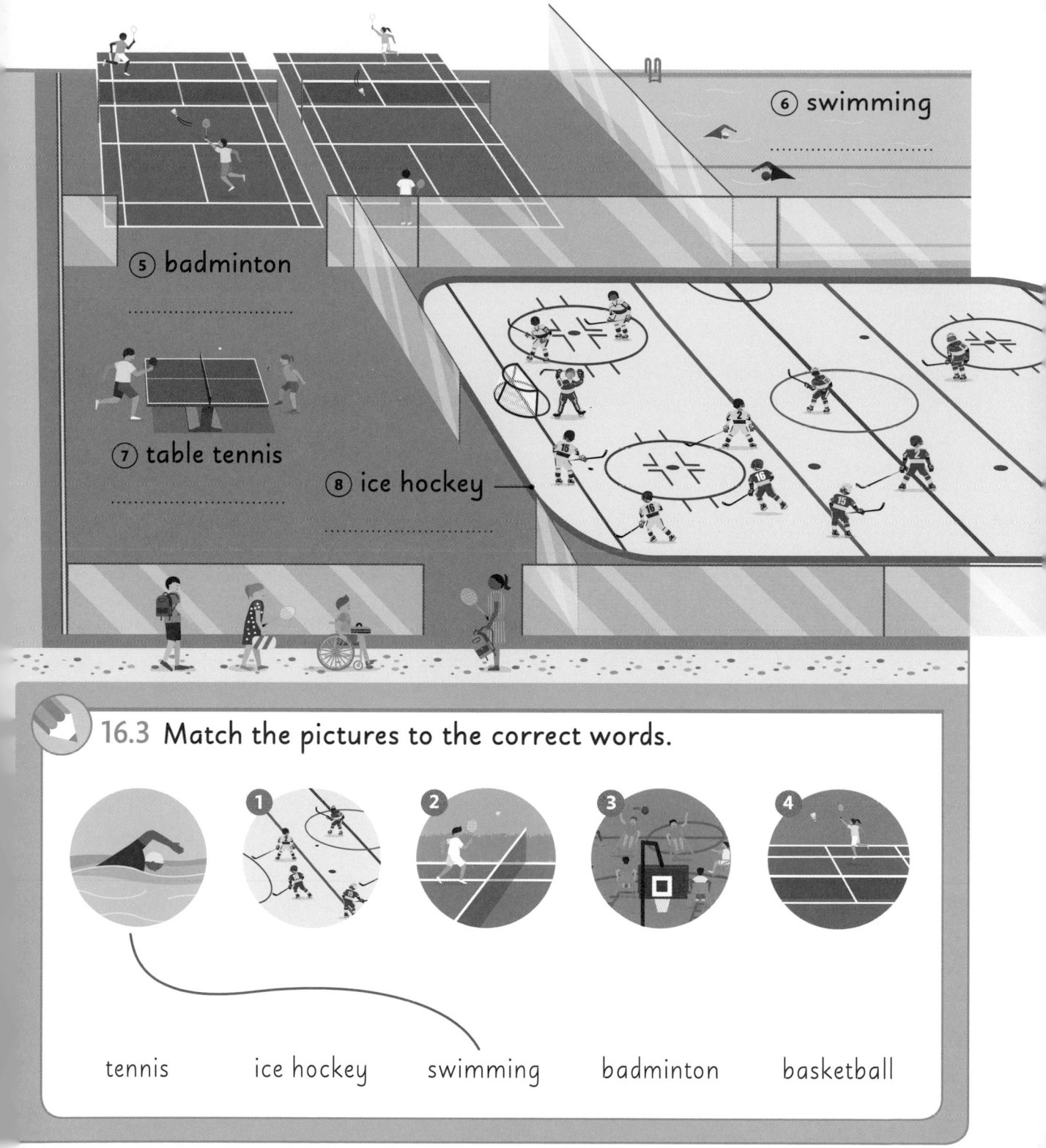
⑤ badminton
⑥ swimming
⑦ table tennis
⑧ ice hockey
16.3 Match the pictures to the correct words.
1
2
3
4
tennis
ice hockey
swimming
badminton
basketball

16.4 Look at the pictures and check off the correct words.

- badminton ☐
- ice hockey ☑
- tennis ☐

1

- table tennis ☐
- badminton ☐
- swimming ☐

2

- baseball ☐
- soccer ☐
- basketball ☐

3

- tennis ☐
- baseball ☐
- swimming ☐

Now listen and repeat.

16.5 Look at the pictures and circle the correct words.

basketball / swimming

1 tennis / ice hockey

2 badminton / baseball

3 soccer / swimming

4 table tennis / soccer

Now listen and repeat.

16.6 Listen, point, and repeat.

① run

.....

② jump

.....

③ swim

.....

④ play tennis

.....

⑤ play ice hockey

.....

⑥ catch

.....

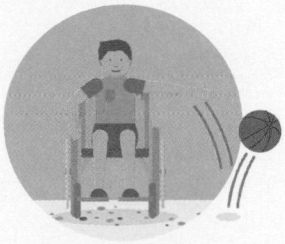

⑦ bounce

.....

⑧ kick

.....

⑨ throw

.....

⑩ hit

.....

16.7 Listen and check off the correct pictures.

A ☐

B ☑

1 A ☐

B ☐

2 A ☐

B ☐

3 A ☐

B ☐

4 A ☐

B ☐

5 A ☐

B ☐

16.8 Look at the pictures and write the letters in the correct order.

j p m u

j u m p

c c h t a

1 c _ _ _ _

s m i w

2 s _ _ _

t o w r h

3 t _ _ _ _

k k c i

4 k _ _ _

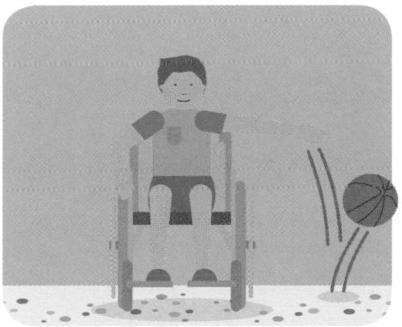

b c n o u e

5 b _ _ _ _ _

Now listen and repeat.

16.9 Listen and read.

I can play basketball.

I	can	play basketball.

Use **can** if you are able to do something.

I	can't	play baseball.

Use **can't** if you are unable to do something.

How it works

Can is a modal verb used to talk about things you are able to do. The negative form is **can't**.

Cannot ➡ Can't

16.10 Listen and check off the correct sentences.

I can play baseball. ☐

I can't play baseball. ☑

1

I can catch a ball. ☐

I can't catch a ball. ☐

2

I can play ice hockey. ☐

I can't play ice hockey. ☐

3

I can hit a ball. ☐

I can't hit a ball. ☐

4

I can swim. ☐

I can't swim. ☐

5

I can play table tennis. ☐

I can't play table tennis. ☐

16.11 Listen and read.

Can you catch a ball?

Can you | **catch a ball?**

Use **Can you** to ask someone if they are able to do something.

Yes, | **I can.**

If you are able to do it, say **Yes** or **Yes, I can**.

No, | **I can't.**

If you are unable to do something, say **No** or **No, I can't**.

How it works

To ask someone a question using **can**, first say **Can you**, then add the verb you want to ask the person about.

16.12 Look at the pictures and write the correct words in the spaces.

Can you | ~~ice hockey~~ | I can. | I can't.

Can you play ice hockey ?

No, I can't.

1 Can you play soccer?

Yes, _____

2 _____ play baseball?

Yes, I can.

3 Can you play basketball?

No, _____

Now listen and repeat.

16.13 Listen and read.

Can she play tennis?

Use **Can she** or **Can he** to ask someone if another person is able to do something.

Can | she / he | play tennis?

Yes, | she can.

If the person is able to do it, say **Yes** or **Yes, she can**.

No, | he can't.

If the person is unable to do something, say **No** or **No, he can't**.

How it works

To ask whether another person is able to do something, say **Can**, followed by **she** or **he**. To reply, say **Yes, she can** or **No, he can't**. You do not need to add an **s** to **can** after **she** or **he**.

16.14 Listen and write the correct answers in the spaces.

No, she can't. ~~No, he can't.~~ Yes, she can. Yes, he can.

Can Andy play tennis?

No, he can't.

1 Can Sara play badminton?

2 Can Sofia play ice hockey?

3 Can Max play table tennis?

17 At the food market

onions
carrots
⑯ potatoes
⑰ meat
⑱ fish
⑳ vegetables
17.3 Write the correct words next to the pictures.
f i s h
1
2
3
4
5

17.4 Read the words and check off the correct pictures.

watermelon A ☑ B ☐

1 banana A ☐ B ☐

2 mangoes A ☐ B ☐

3 pineapple A ☐ B ☐

4 potatoes A ☐ B ☐

Now listen and repeat.

17.5 Look at the pictures and write the correct words in the spaces.

fish coconut ~~meat~~
orange lime carrot

meat

1 _____

2 _____

3 _____

4 _____

5 _____

Now listen and repeat.

17.6 Listen and color in the pictures.

1

2

3

4

5

17.7 Listen and sing.

Apples and oranges,
pears and mangoes, too.
Here are nice potatoes,
and meat and fish for you.

17.8 Listen and read.

I like oranges and pears.

I like | **oranges** | **and** | **pears.**

To talk about things you enjoy, use **like**.

Use **and** to talk about two or more things.

I don't like | **bananas** | **or** | **watermelons.**

To make the sentence negative, put **don't** before **like**.

Use **or** when talking about two or more things in a negative sentence.

How it works

I like is an example of the **present simple** form of the verb **to like**. Add **don't** before **like** to make the sentence negative. **And** and **or** are conjunctions. Use **and** in positive sentences and **or** in negative sentences.

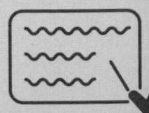

17.9 Listen to Andy and circle the correct words.

I like / don't like oranges and pears.

1 I like / don't like watermelons.

2 I like / don't like apples.

3 I like / don't like lemons and limes.

4 I like / don't like carrots or onions.

5 I like / don't like tomatoes.

17.10 Listen and read.

Do you like apples?

Do you like apples?

Say this to ask someone if they like something.

Yes, I do.

You can answer **Yes** or **Yes, I do.**

No, I don't.

You can answer **No** or **No, I don't.**

How it works

To ask someone a question in the **present simple**, put **Do you** before the verb.

Some words form the plural differently from most nouns. If the name of the fruit or vegetable ends with an **o**, add **es** to the singular form rather than just **s**.

Tomato → Tomatoes
Potato → Potatoes
Mango → Mangoes

17.11 Look at the pictures and write the correct words in the spaces.

I don't. ~~Do you~~ I do. like

Now listen and repeat.

17.12 Listen and read.

May I have a mango, please?

May I have | a | mango, please?

Say this to ask someone to give you something.

Use **a** or **an** if you're asking for one thing.

May I have | some | kiwis, please?

Use **some** if you're asking for two or more things.

How it works

May I have is the question used to ask for something.

A, **an**, and **some** are indefinite articles. Use indefinite articles when you don't want to talk about a specific example of a thing. Put **a** or **an** in front of singular nouns, and **some** in front of plural nouns.

17.13 Look at the pictures and write the correct words in the spaces.

an ~~some~~ a some

May I have ___some___ kiwis, please?

1 May I have _____ banana, please?

2 May I have _____ orange, please?

3 May I have _____ vegetables, please?

Now listen and repeat.

18 At the toy store

18.1 Listen, point, and repeat.
18.2 How many stars are there?

18.3 Match the pictures to the correct words.

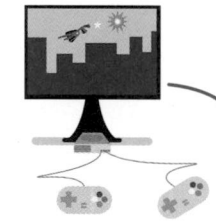

the moon

video game

1

robot

2

puppet

3

TOYS
9 rocket
10 the moon
11 stars
12 robot
13 balloons
14 train
15 video game
16 board game
It's Ben's birthday.
Let's give him a robot.
TOYS

18.4 Look at the pictures and check off the correct words.

- teddy bear ☑
- robot ☐
- train ☐

1

- board game ☐
- monster ☐
- video game ☐

2

- the moon ☐
- puppet ☐
- car ☐

3

- action figure ☐
- ball ☐
- rocket ☐

Now listen and repeat.

18.5 Write the correct words next to the pictures.

rocket | ~~the moon~~ | alien | robot

t h e m o o n

1 _ _ _ _ _

2 _ _ _ _ _ _

3 _ _ _ _ _

Now listen and repeat.

18.6 Look at the pictures and write the correct words in the spaces.

stars ~~puppets~~ monster action figure

What are those?

They're puppets.

1 What's that?

It's a _____.

2 What are those?

They're _____.

3 What's that?

It's an _____.

Now listen and repeat.

18.7 Listen and read.

Sofia likes cars.

Sofia / She — likes — cars.

After **he, she,** or someone's name, put an **s** on the end of **like.**

Ben / He — doesn't like — board games.

To make the sentence negative, put **doesn't** before **like**.

How it works

She likes and **He doesn't like** are examples of the **present simple** form of the verb **to like**. In positive sentences with **he, she,** or someone's name, put an **s** on the end of **like**. To make the sentence negative, put **doesn't** before **like** and don't add an **s**.

18.8 Look at the pictures and write the correct words in the spaces.

rockets ~~cars~~ trains video games

Sofia Eva Ben Sam

Sofia likes cars. Her cousin Eva doesn't like

1 _____. Ben likes 2 _____, but

his friend Sam doesn't like 3 _____.

Now listen and read.

18.9 Listen and write the correct words in the spaces.

likes doesn't like ~~likes~~ doesn't like

Alice likes robots.

1 Hugo _____ puppets.

2 Lucy _____ dolls.

3 Emma _____ monsters.

18.10 Listen and read.

Does he like trains?

Does he | **like** | **trains?**

To form a question, put **Does** before **he**, **she**, or someone's name.

Then add **like.** Don't add an **s** to the verb when you use it in a question.

Yes, | **he does.**

Answer **Yes** or **Yes, he does.**

No, | **he doesn't.**

Answer **No** or **No, he doesn't.**

How it works

To ask a question with **he** or **she**, start the question with **Does**, not **Do**. Do not add an **s** to **like**.

18.11 Listen and check off the correct answers.

Does he like robots?

Yes, he does. ☑
No, he doesn't. ☐

1 

Does she like dolls?

Yes, she does. ☐
No, she doesn't. ☐

2 

Does he like video games?

Yes, he does. ☐
No, he doesn't. ☐

3 

Does she like monsters?

Yes, she does. ☐
No, she doesn't. ☐

4 

Does he like action figures?

Yes, he does. ☐
No, he doesn't. ☐

5 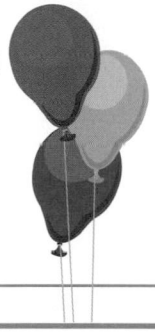

Does she like balloons?

Yes, she does. ☐
No, she doesn't. ☐

18.12 There are four sentences. Mark the beginning and end of each one and write them below.

Doesheliketrains?/No,hedoesn't.Doesshelikedolls?Yes,shedoes.

Does he like trains?

2 _____

1 _____

3 _____

Now listen and repeat.

18.13 Listen and read.

I love puppets.

I love | puppets.

I love is a much stronger way of saying **I like**.

Me too!

Say this if you feel the same as Sara.

I don't.

Say this if you don't feel the same as Sara.

18.14 Listen and sing.

Maria likes dolls,
but she doesn't like puppets.
Andy likes cars,
but he doesn't like rockets.
I like trains and video games,
and my favorite toy
is my monster!

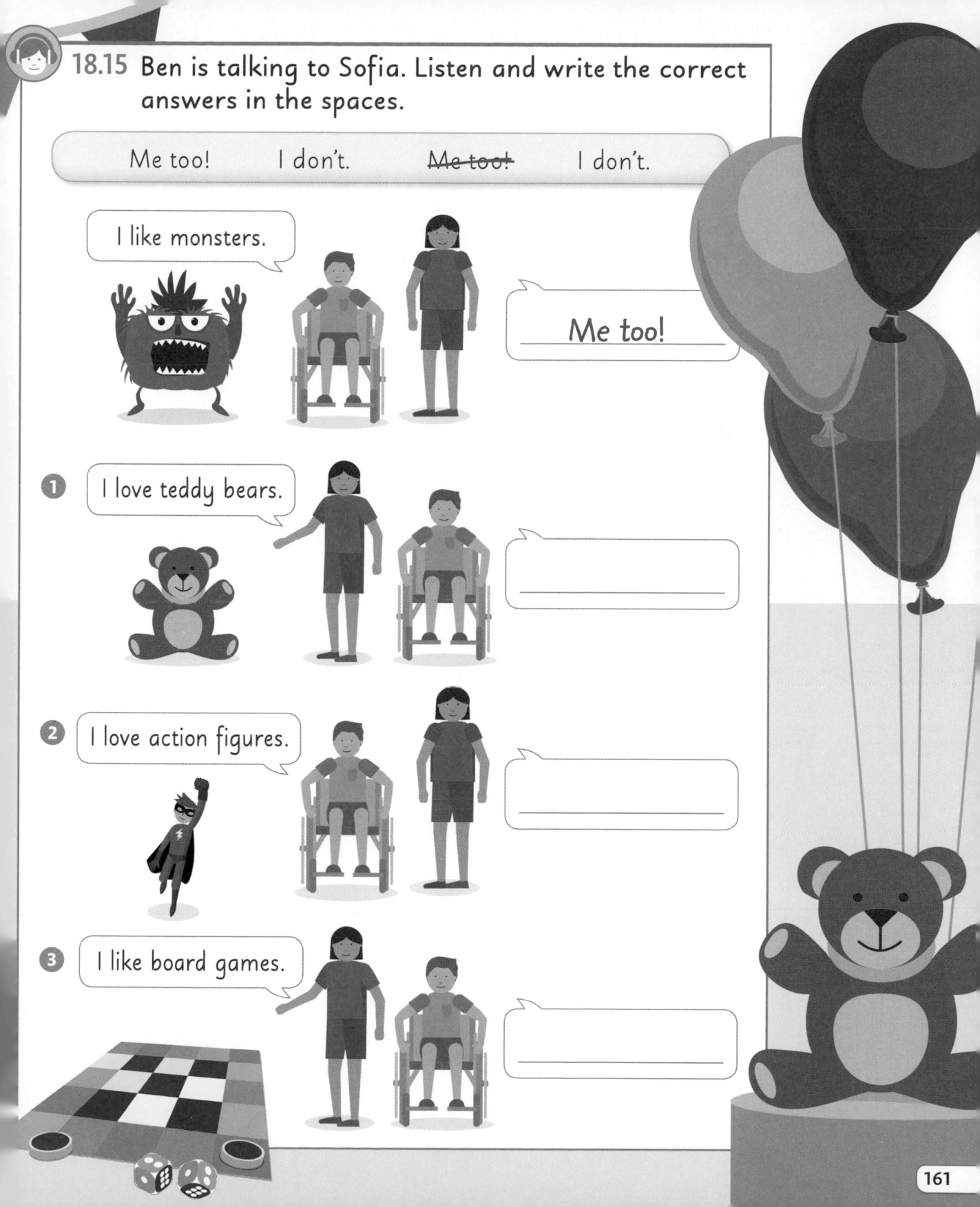

18.15 Ben is talking to Sofia. Listen and write the correct answers in the spaces.

Me too! I don't. ~~Me too!~~ I don't.

I like monsters.

Me too!

1 I love teddy bears.

2 I love action figures.

3 I like board games.

19 Our hobbies

19.1 Listen, point, and repeat.
19.2 Where is Sofia?

19.3 Match the pictures to the correct words.

dance

1 read

2 draw pictures

3 take photos

4 sing

1 ride a bike

.....

2 watch soccer

.....

3 skateboard

.....

4 draw pictures

.....

I enjoy painting.

5 paint

.....

Me too. It's fun!

⑥ read
⑦ sing
⑧ dance
⑨ play the guitar
⑩ play the piano
⑪ take photos

19.4 Listen and check off the correct pictures.

A ☐ B ☑

1 A ☐ B ☐

2 A ☐ B ☐

3 A ☐ B ☐

4 A ☐ B ☐

5 A ☐ B ☐

19.5 Look at the pictures and write the correct words in the spaces.

paint ~~play the guitar~~ play the piano
sing ride a bike take photos

play the guitar

1 _____

2 _____

3 _____

4 _____

5 _____

Now listen and repeat.

19.6 Listen and read.

I like playing the piano.

I like | playing the piano.

Add **ing** to the verb after **like**.

I enjoy | dancing.

You can also say **I enjoy** to say you like doing an activity.

I don't like | painting.

To make the sentence negative, add **don't** before **like**.

How it works

To say how you feel about an activity, say **I like** or **I don't like**, followed by the **ing** form of the verb.

If a verb ends in **e**, like **dance**, remove the **e** and add **ing**.

19.7 Listen and match the names to the correct pictures.

Sofia

1 James

2 Kim

3 Bill

4 Tom

drawing

painting

reading

singing

watching soccer

19.8 Rewrite the sentences in the correct order.

don't | reading. | like | I

I don't like reading.

1 enjoy | I | taking photos.

2 riding a bike. | like | I | don't

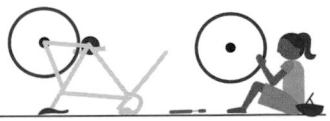

3 I | watching soccer. | like

Now listen and repeat.

19.9 Listen and read.

Do you like singing?

Do you like | singing?

To ask if someone likes an activity, put **Do you** before **like**.

Then add **ing** to the verb.

Yes, | I do.

You can answer **Yes** or **Yes, I do**.

No, | I don't.

You can answer **No** or **No, I don't**.

How it works

To ask someone if someone likes an activity, first say **Do you like**, then add **ing** to the verb.

19.10 Andy and Sofia are talking. Listen and check off the correct answers.

Do you like singing?

Yes, I do. ☑

No, I don't. ☐

1 Do you like playing the guitar?

Yes, I do. ☐

No, I don't. ☐

2 Do you like dancing?

Yes, I do. ☐

No, I don't. ☐

3 Do you like painting?

Yes, I do. ☐

No, I don't. ☐

4 Do you like riding a bike?

Yes, I do. ☐

No, I don't. ☐

19.11 Listen and sing.

Do you have hobbies?
Yes, I do.
I love reading books
and skateboarding, too.

Do you like playing tennis?
Yes, I do.
I love playing tennis
and playing soccer, too.

Do you enjoy singing?
Yes, I do.
I love singing songs,
and I love dancing, too.

20 Review: What I like

20.1 Listen and read.

My name's Sofia. I like skateboarding and trains. I don't like painting. I can play tennis and swim. I can't play the piano.
I like mangoes, but I don't like apples.

My friend Max likes cars. He doesn't like board games. He likes oranges, but he doesn't like bananas.

20.2 Write about the things you and a friend like and draw a picture.

My name's _____.

I like _____ and _____.

I don't like _____. I can _____

and _____. I can't _____.

I like _____, but I don't like _____.

My friend likes _____.

My friend doesn't like _____.

21 Our party clothes

21.3 Write the correct words next to the pictures.

s h i r t

1 _ _ _

2 _ _ _ _ _ _

3 _ _ _

⑩ baseball cap .....

⑪ jeans .....

⑫ shoe .....

⑬ boot .....

⑭ glasses .....

⑮ shirt .....

⑯ bag .....

⑰ jacket .....

21.4 Match the pictures to the correct words.

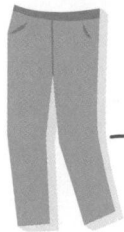

dress

1 

pants

2 

boot

3 

watch

4 

baseball cap

5 

glasses

Now listen and repeat.

21.5 Read the sentences and check off the correct pictures.

It's a hat. A ☐  B ☑ 

1 It's a shirt. A ☐  B ☐ 

2 They're jeans. A ☐ 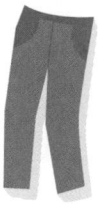 B ☐ 

3 It's a purse. A ☐  B ☐ 

4 They're shorts. A ☐  B ☐ 

Now listen and repeat.

21.6 Look at the pictures and write the correct answers in the spaces.

It's a watch. It's a sock. ~~It's a skirt.~~ It's a t-shirt. It's a jacket. It's a shoe.

What's this?

It's a skirt.

1 What's this?

2 What's this?

3 What's this?

4 What's this?

5 What this?

Now listen and repeat.

21.7 Listen and sing.

We're at a party,
so let's all dance and play.
What a fun party
for Ben's birthday!

Andy's wearing his
favorite t-shirt,
and Sara has
a beautiful skirt.

21.8 Listen and read.

It's my party!
I'm wearing a hat.

I'm wearing shorts.

I'm wearing a hat.

I'm wearing a hat.

To say what you are wearing now, say **I'm**, followed by the verb with **ing** at its end.

I'm wearing shorts.

Some items of clothing, such as **shorts**, **pants**, or **glasses**, use the plural form.

How it works

These are examples of the **present continuous** form of the verb **to wear**. Use the **present continuous** to talk about doing something in the present moment.

21.9 Listen and check off the correct pictures.

A ☑

B ☐

1 A ☐

B ☐

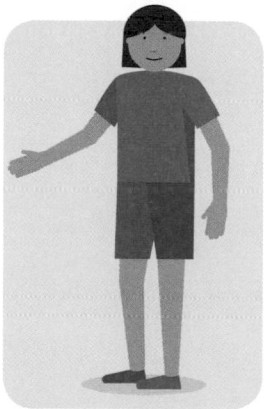

2 A ☐

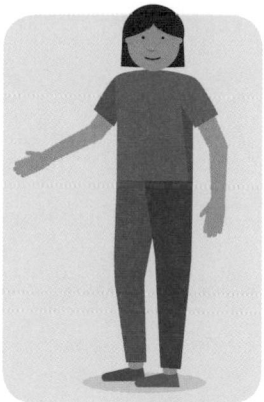

B ☐

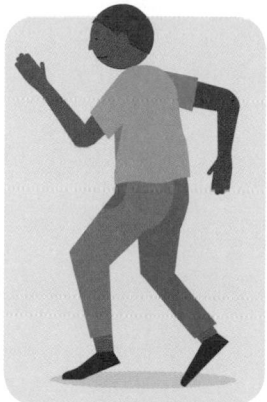

3 A ☐

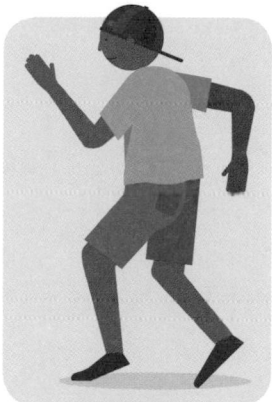

B ☐

4 A ☐

B ☐

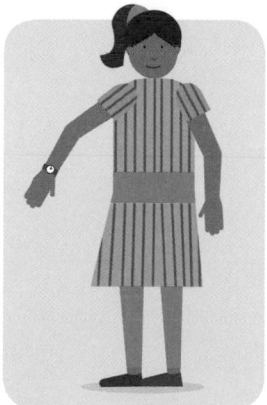

5 A ☐

B ☐

21.10 Listen and read.

Are you wearing my shoes?

Are you **wearing** **my shoes?**

To ask someone a question, put **Are you** before the verb.

Add **ing** to the verb.

Yes, **I am.**

If you're wearing the item, you can say **Yes** or **Yes, I am.**

No, **I'm not.**

If you're not wearing the item, you can say **No** or **No, I'm not.**

How it works

To ask a question in the **present continuous**, put **Are you** before the **ing** form of the verb.

21.11 Look at the pictures and check off the correct answers.

Are you wearing my hat?

- Yes, I am. ☐
- No, I'm not. ☑

1. Are you wearing my jacket?

- Yes, I am. ☐
- No, I'm not. ☐

2. Are you wearing my watch?

- Yes, I am. ☐
- No, I'm not. ☐

3. Are you wearing my glasses?

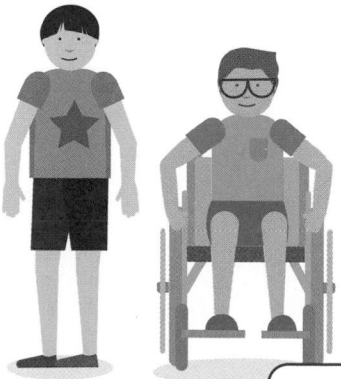

- Yes, I am. ☐
- No, I'm not. ☐

Now listen and repeat.

21.12 Listen and read.

What a beautiful dress!

What a nice t-shirt!

What a big hat!

What dirty shoes!

What a beautiful dress!

What a | beautiful | dress!

Say **What a**, followed by a describing word (an adjective).

What | dirty | shoes!

To describe two or more things, just say **What**.

How it works

To explain or emphasize what you think of something, put **What a** before an adjective and noun. To describe two or more things, just say **What**.

21.13 Look at the pictures and write the correct words in the spaces.

What a ~~What a~~ What a
What a What What

What a clean t-shirt!

1 _____ beautiful boots!

2 _____ dirty sock!

3 _____ nice glasses!

4 _____ nice shirt!

5 _____ big purse!

Now listen and repeat.

22 Our day at the beach

22.1 Listen, point, and repeat.
22.2 How many balls are there?

① seagull

.....

② ship

.....

③ surf

.....

④ jellyfish

.....

⑤ fly a kite

.....

⑥ sand

.....

⑦ play soccer

.....

⑧ bucket

.....

⑨ shovel

.....

⑩ listen to music

.....

⑪ drink juice

.....

Maria's eating ice cream.

Sofia's drinking juice.

⑫ eat ice cream

.....

13 fish
swim in the ocean
15 run on the beach
16 read a book
17 throw a ball
18 shell
22.3 Match the pictures to the correct words.
play soccer
1
surf
2
drink juice
3
listen to music
4
read a book
5
throw a ball

22.4 Look at the pictures and write the correct answers in the spaces.

It's a seagull. ~~It's a jellyfish.~~ It's a shovel.
It's a shell. It's a ship. It's a bucket.

What's this?

It's a jellyfish.

1 What's this?

_____

2 What's this?

_____

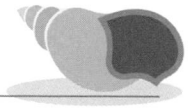

3 What's this?

_____

4 What's this?

_____

5 What's this?

_____

Now listen and repeat.

22.5 Listen and check off the correct pictures.

A ☐

B ☑

1 A ☐

B ☐

2 A ☐

B ☐

3 A ☐

B ☐

4 A ☐

B ☐

5 A ☐

B ☐

22.6 Look at the pictures and write the letters in the correct order.

s i p h

s h i p

b k c u e t

1 b _ _ _ _ _ _

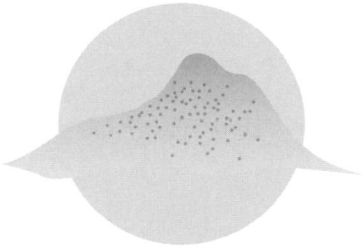

s a d n

2 s _ _ _

r n u

3 r _ _

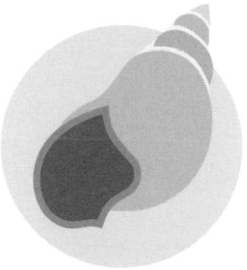

s l e h l

4 s _ _ _ _ _

s i m w

5 s _ _ _

Now listen and repeat.

22.7 Listen and read.

He's listening to music.

He's listening to music.

Add **is** or **'s** after **she**, **he**, or someone's name.

Add **ing** to the main verb.

She isn't listening to music.

Put **isn't** before the main verb to make the sentence negative.

How it works

These are examples of the **present continuous**. To make the present continuous with **he**, **she**, or a person's name, add **is** or **'s**, followed by the **ing** form of the verb.

22.8 Look at the pictures and check off the correct answers.

He's listening to music. ☑
He isn't listening to music. ☐

1 She's swimming. ☐
She isn't swimming. ☐

2 He's flying a kite. ☐
He isn't flying a kite. ☐

3 She's drinking juice. ☐
She isn't drinking juice. ☐

Now listen and repeat.

22.9 Listen and match the names to the correct pictures.

Nick 1 May 2 Pat 3 Mark 4 Lucy

swimming

throwing a ball

fishing

playing soccer

flying a kite

22.10 Listen and read.

Is she eating ice cream?

Is she **eating ice cream?**

Add **Is** before **she**, **he**, or someone's name.

Add **ing** to the main verb.

Yes, **she is.**

Answer **Yes** or **Yes, she is.**

No, **she isn't.**

Answer **No** or **No, she isn't.**

How it works

To make a question in the **present continuous**, put **is** before **he**, **she**, or the person's name, followed by the **ing** form of the main verb.

22.11 Look at the pictures and write the correct answers in the spaces.

Yes, he is. ~~No, he isn't.~~ Yes, she is. No, she isn't.

Now listen and repeat.

23 Lunchtime

23.3 Write the correct words under the pictures.

r i c e

1 ___ ___ ___

2 ___ ___ ___ ___ ___

3 ___ ___ ___ ___

⑩ chocolate

.....

⑪ noodles

.....

⑫ drinks

.....

⑬ fruit

.....

⑭ juice

.....

⑮ water

.....

⑯ lemonade

.....

23.4 Look at the pictures and circle the correct words.

sausages / pie

1 

cake / orange

2 

chocolate / fruit

3 

juice / noodles

4 

rice / candy

5 

burger / salad

Now listen and repeat.

23.5 Listen and check off the correct pictures.

A ☐ B ☑

1 

A ☐ B ☐

2 

A ☐ B ☐

3 

A ☐ B ☐

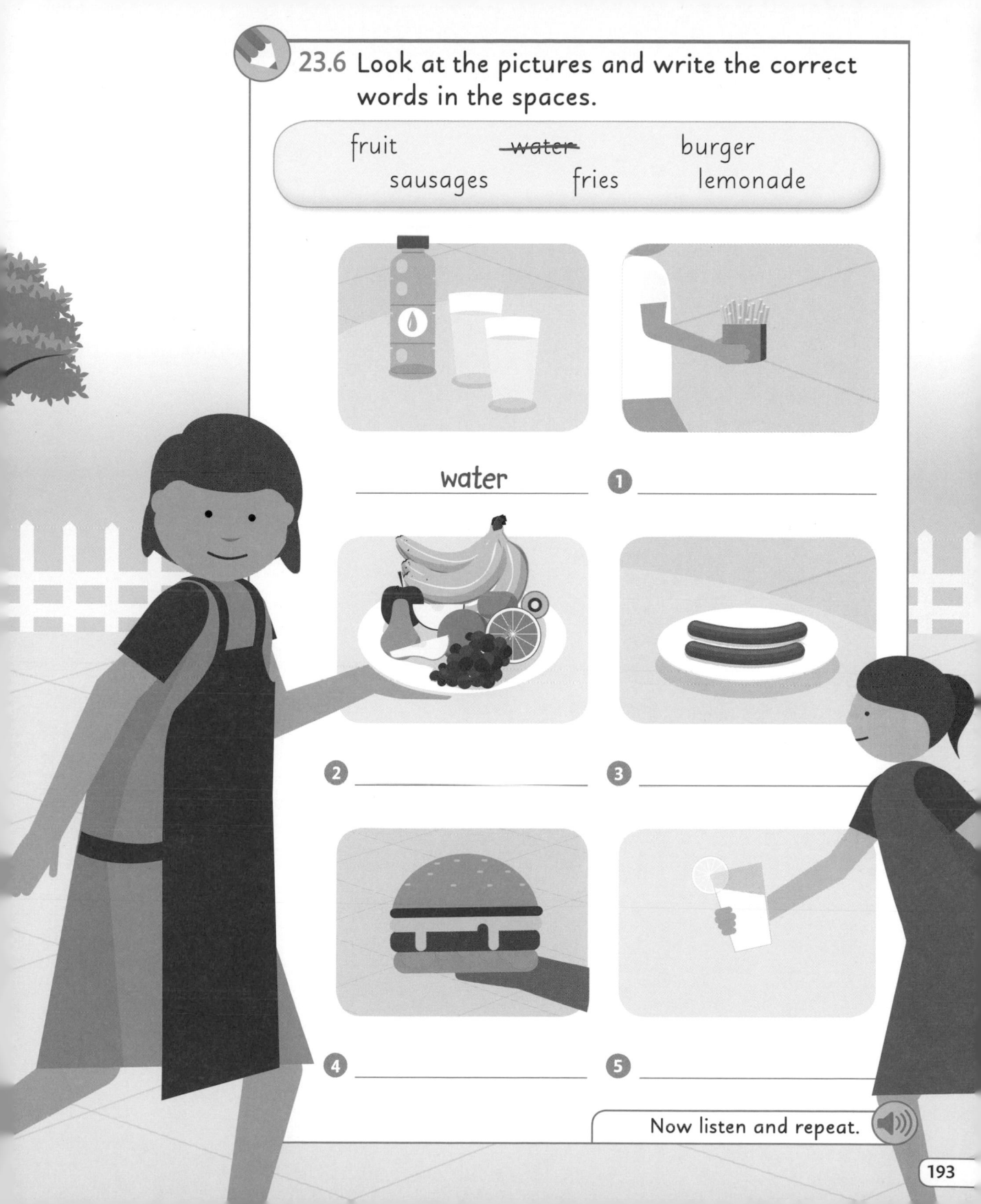

23.6 Look at the pictures and write the correct words in the spaces.

fruit ~~water~~ burger
sausages fries lemonade

water

1 _____

2 _____

3 _____

4 _____

5 _____

Now listen and repeat.

23.7 Listen and read.

What would you like?

What would you like?

This is a polite way of asking someone what they want.

I'd like | a burger, | please.

This is a polite way of saying **I want**.

Add **please** to be polite.

I'd like | some rice, | please.

Use **some** if you're asking for two or more things, or for something that is uncountable.

How it works

I'd like is a polite way of requesting something. Using **I want** for a request may seem rude in English.

Some things cannot be counted individually. These are called uncountables. Use **some** when asking for plural things or something that is uncountable.

I would ➡ **I'd**

23.8 Listen and match the names to the correct pictures.

Ben ❶ Alex ❷ Eva ❸ Grace ❹ Mark

fries

rice

orange

salad

noodles

23.9 Rewrite the sentences in the correct order.

please. a burger, I'd like

I'd like a burger, please.

❶ drink, a I'd like please.

❷ some lemonade, please. I'd like

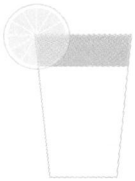

❸ please. some I'd like fruit,

Now listen and repeat.

23.10 Listen and read.

Would you like an ice cream?

Would you like | an ice cream?

Use this to ask if someone wants something.

Yes, please.

This a polite way of saying **yes**.

No, thank you.

This a polite way of saying **no**.

Would you like | some juice?

Yes, I would.

This is another way of saying **yes**.

No, I wouldn't

This is another way of saying **no**.

How it works

Would you like is a polite way of asking someone if they want something. It is important to use **please** and **thank you** in your answers.

Would not ➡ **Wouldn't**

23.11 Listen and check off the correct answers.

Would you like some juice?

- Yes, I would. ☑
- No, I wouldn't. ☐

1. Would you like some fruit?

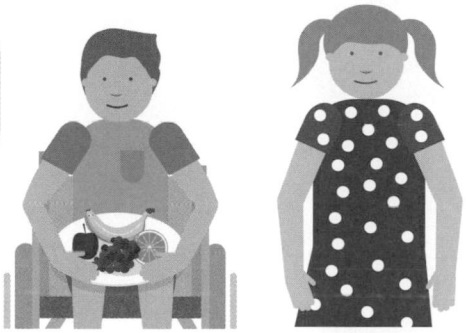

- Yes, please. ☐
- No, thank you. ☐

2. Would you like a burger?

- Yes, please. ☐
- No, thank you. ☐

3. Would you like a salad?

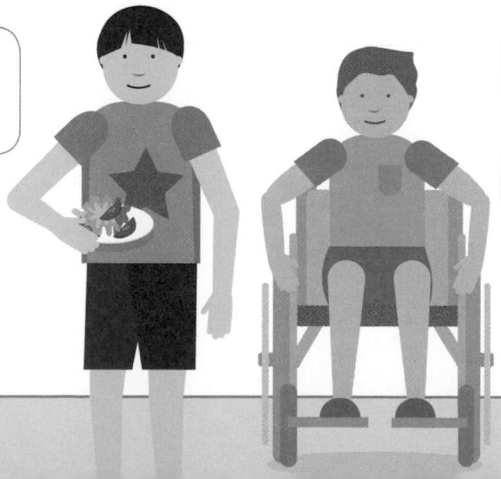

- Yes, I would. ☐
- No, I wouldn't. ☐

23.12 Listen, point, and repeat.

23.13 Listen and read.

What's for lunch today?

What's for

breakfast?

lunch?

dinner?

Say this to ask about a meal.

23.14 Listen and check off the correct pictures.

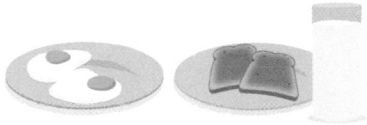

A ☐ B ☑

1 A ☐ B ☐

2 A ☐ B ☐

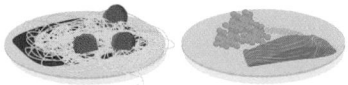

3 A ☐ B ☐

4 A ☐ B ☐

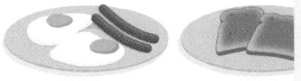

5 A ☐ B ☐

24 At the park

24.1 Listen, point, and repeat.
24.2 What are Sara and Max playing?

24.3 Write the correct words under the pictures.
g i r l
1
2
3
6 person
7 people
8 child/kid
9 children/kids
11 men
10 man

24.4 Look at the pictures and circle the correct words.

woman / women

1 person / people

2 boy / girl

3 child / children

4 man / men

5 woman / baby

Now listen and repeat.

24.5 Find and circle the five words in the grid.

girl

~~child~~

people

kid

person

boy

p	e	r	s	o	n
e	c	h	i	l	d
o	s	i	g	e	b
p	b	k	i	d	o
l	y	r	r	d	y
e	o	h	l	i	h

24.6 Look at the pictures and write the letters in the correct order.

c d l i h

c h i l d

w n a o m

1 w _ _ _ _ _

m n e

2 m _ _ _

g r l i

3 g _ _ _

w n e m o

4 w _ _ _ _ _

k d s i

5 k _ _ _

Now listen and repeat.

24.7 Listen and read.

Is this Max's bag?

Is this | Max's | bag?

To show that someone owns something, add **'s** after their name.

Max's | bag | is blue.

How it works

These sentences use the possessive apostrophe. We place it before an **s** to show that a person owns something.

24.8 Listen and match the person to the correct thing.

Max | 1 Matt | 2 Sam | 3 Kim | 4 Ann

red bike

blue bag

green bike

yellow bag

orange bike

24.9 Look at the pictures and write the correct words in the spaces.

woman's ~~Sara's~~ boy's Andy's girl's baby's

Sara's book is blue.

1 The _____ ball is red.

2 The _____ doll is pink.

3 The _____ dog is dirty.

4 _____ bike is yellow.

5 The _____ skirt is black.

Now listen and repeat.

24.10 Listen and read.

Whose ball is this?

Whose | ball | is this?

Say this to ask who owns something.

Add **is this** to finish the question.

It's | mine.

This means the ball belongs to me.

How it works

Whose is a question word used to ask who owns something.
Mine is an example of a possessive pronoun. These are used to say who owns something.

24.11 Listen and read.

It's mine.

It's yours.

The ball belongs to you.

It's his.

The ball belongs to him.

It's hers.

The ball belongs to her.

It's ours.

The ball belongs to our group.

It's yours.

The ball belongs to more than one of you.

It's theirs.

The ball belongs to them.

24.12 Listen and write the correct answers in the spaces.

It's his. ~~It's mine.~~ It's theirs.
It's ours. It's hers. It's yours.

Whose ball is this?

It's mine.

1 Whose dog is this?

2 Whose bike is this?

3 Whose boat is this?

4 Whose lunch is this?

5 Whose doll is this?

25 My day

25.1 Listen, point, and repeat.
25.2 Who is Max calling?

① I get up.

.....

⑫ I go to sleep.

.....

25.3 Match the pictures to the correct sentences.

I study English. I eat lunch. I go home.

⑪ I eat dinner.

.....

⑩ I go swimming.

.....

⑨ I call my friend.

.....

② I make my bed.
③ I eat breakfast.
④ I brush my teeth.
3
4
5
I go to sleep.
I make my bed.
I get up.
⑤ I walk to school.
⑥ I study English.
⑦ I eat lunch.
⑧ I go home.

25.4 Listen and check off the correct pictures.

A ☐ B ☑

1 A ☐ B ☐

2 A ☐ B ☐

3 A ☐ B ☐

4 A ☐ B ☐

5 A ☐ B ☐

25.5 There are four sentences. Mark the beginning and end of each one and write them below.

I go home.

1 _____

2 _____

3 _____

Igohome. | Igetup. Igotosleep. Ieatlunch.

Now listen and repeat.

25.6 Look at the pictures and write the correct sentences in the spaces.

I eat breakfast. I eat lunch. I study English.
I brush my teeth. I walk to school. ~~I make my bed.~~

I make my bed.

1 _____

2 _____

3 _____

4 _____

5 _____

Now listen and repeat.

25.7 Listen and read.

What time is it?

What time is it?

This is the question you ask to find out the time.

It's **ten o'clock.**

Answer the question by saying **It's** plus the time.

To say what time it is, you say the number, followed by **o'clock**.

25.8 Match the clocks to the correct times.

It's six o'clock. It's two o'clock. It's eleven o'clock. It's seven o'clock.

Now listen and repeat.

25.9 Listen, point, and repeat.

① In the morning ..... ② In the afternoon ..... ③ In the evening ..... ④ At night .....

25.10 Listen and check off the correct answers.

I go to school in the morning. ☑

I go to school at night. ☐

1

I study English at night. ☐

I study English in the afternoon. ☐

2

I call my friend in the evening. ☐

I call my friend in the afternoon. ☐

3

I go to sleep in the morning. ☐

I go to sleep at night. ☐

25.11 Listen and read.

When do you brush your teeth?

When do you | brush your teeth?

Use this to ask at what time of day a person does something.

I brush my teeth | in the morning. / at seven o'clock.

You can answer saying the part of day.

To say the time you do something, say **at**, followed by the time.

25.12 Read the sentences and write the correct words in the spaces.

breakfast ~~morning~~ go to sleep walk six o'clock we

In the morning, I wake up at seven o'clock.

1 I eat _____, and then I brush my teeth.

2 I _____ to school at eight o'clock.

3 In the afternoon, _____ study English.

4 I eat dinner at _____ with my family.

5 Then I _____ at seven o'clock.

Now listen and repeat.

25.13 Listen and read.

Max walks to school.

He
Max
She

walks to school.

Remember to add **s** to the verb after **he**, **she**, or a person's name.

I
We
You
They

walk to school.

You do not need to add an **s** after **I**, **we**, **you**, or **they**.

How it works

These sentences include examples of the **present simple.** The present simple is used to talk things that we do often or everyday.

25.14 Look at the pictures and circle the correct words.

Max **walk** / **walks** to school.

1 They **eat** / **eats** lunch.

2 We **go** / **goes** swimming.

3 She **study** / **studies** English.

4 She **get** / **gets** up.

5 Max **make** / **makes** his bed.

Now listen and repeat.

25.15 Listen, point, and repeat.

Monday ① Monday .....

Tuesday ② Tuesday .....

Wednesday ③ Wednesday .....

Thursday ④ Thursday .....

Friday ⑤ Friday .....

Saturday ⑥ Saturday .....

Sunday ⑦ Sunday .....

25.16 Listen and read.

I go swimming on Fridays.

I go swimming | on Fridays.

Say **on**, followed by the day of the week with an **s** at its end.

So do I.

Say this if you also go swimming on Fridays.

I don't.

Say this if you don't go swimming on Fridays.

How it works

Use **at** when talking about what time you do something. Use **on** when talking about what days you do something.

25.17 Listen and check off the correct answers.

I go swimming on Fridays.

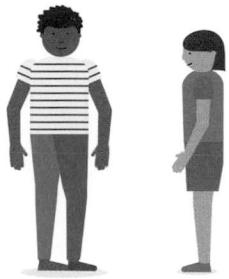

So do I. ☑

I don't. ☐

1. I go home at two o'clock.

So do I. ☐

I don't. ☐

2. I eat breakfast at eight o'clock.

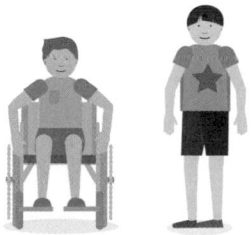

So do I. ☐

I don't. ☐

3. I call my friend on Thursdays.

So do I. ☐

I don't. ☐

26 Review: Me and my day

26.1 Listen and read.

I'm Andy. I have black hair and brown eyes. Today I'm wearing shorts and a t-shirt.

I like school. I go to school at 8 o'clock. In the morning, I study English. I eat rice and beans for lunch, and I drink juice. I go home at 3 o'clock. In the evening, I call my friends. I eat dinner at 6 o'clock, and I go to sleep at 7 o'clock.

26.2 Write about your day and draw what you're wearing.

I'm _____. I have _____ hair and _____ eyes. Today I'm wearing _____ and _____.

I _____ school. I go to school at _____. In the morning, I study _____. I eat _____ for lunch, and I drink _____. I go home at _____. In the evening, I _____. I eat dinner at _____, and I go to sleep at _____.

The alphabet

A1 The English alphabet has 26 letters. Listen to the audio and repeat each letter. Then listen to the song and sing.

Use a capital letter for the first letter of a sentence, people's names, and the days of the week.

Use lower-case letters the rest of the time.

Aa Bb Cc

Dd Ee Ff Gg Hh

Ii Jj Kk Ll Mm

Nn Oo Pp Qq Rr

Ss Tt Uu Vv Ww

Xx Yy Zz

Handwriting guide

A2 To practice writing English letters, start at the red dot and then follow the arrows.

A a

B b

C c

D d

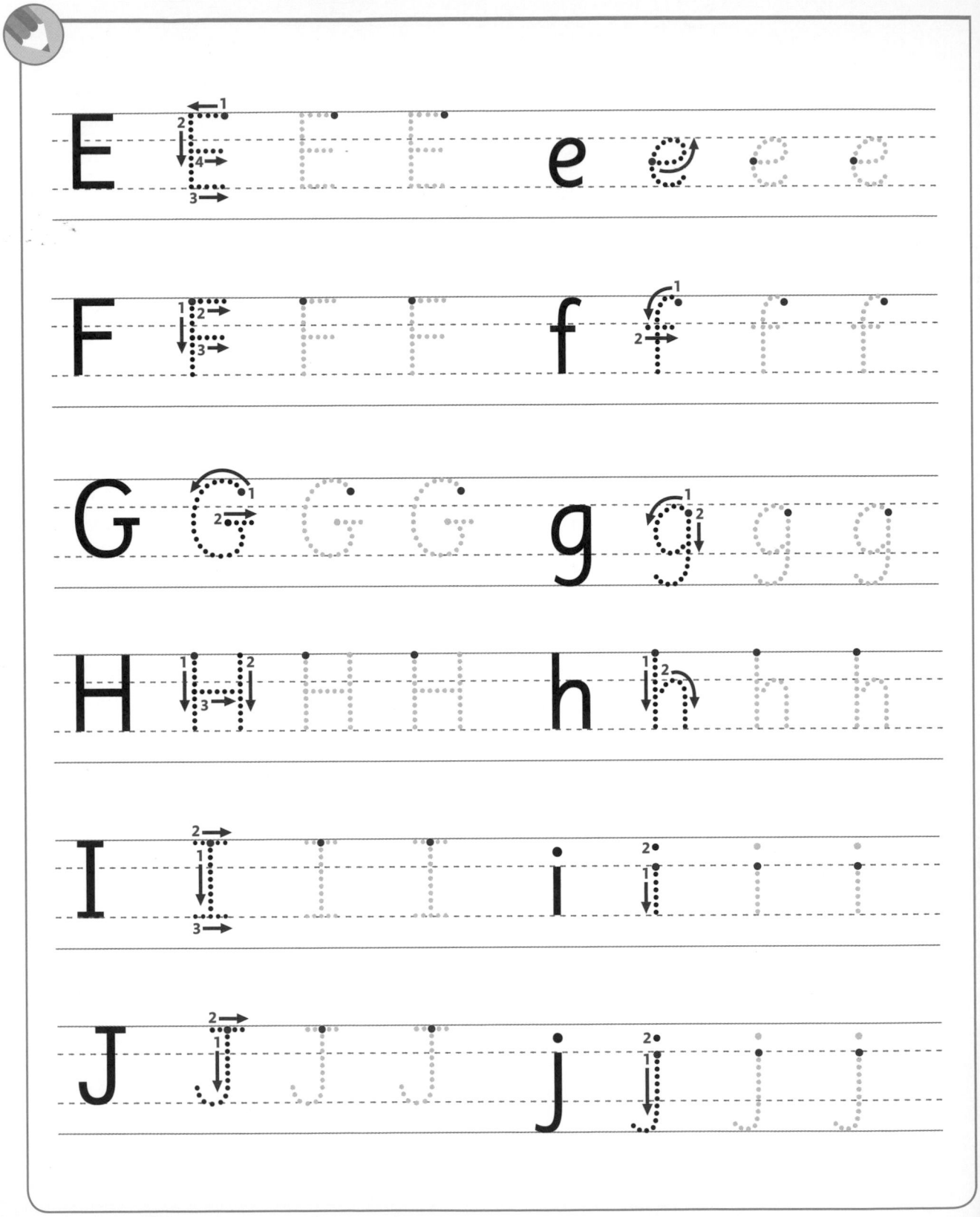
E
e
F
f
G
g
H
h
I
i
J
j

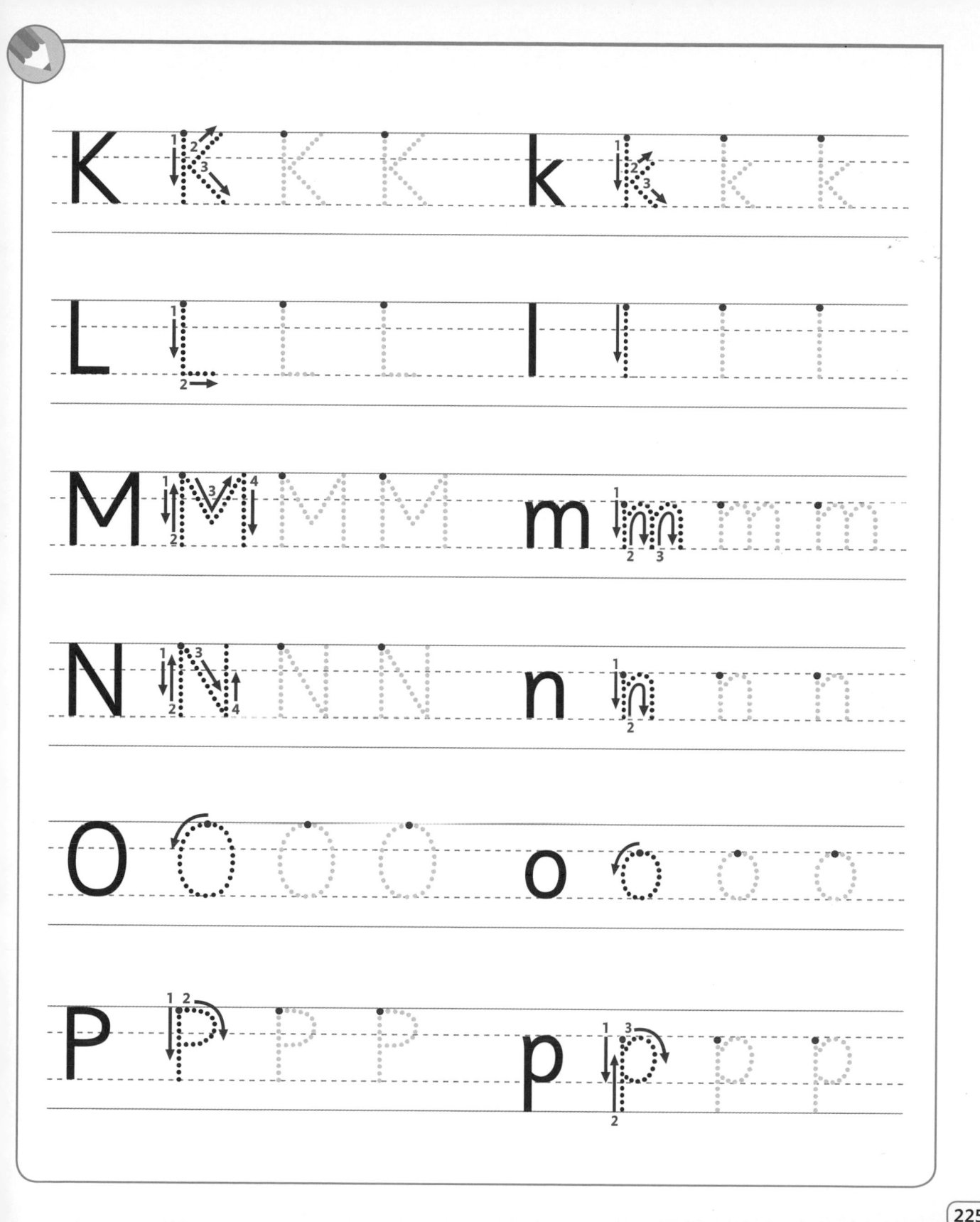

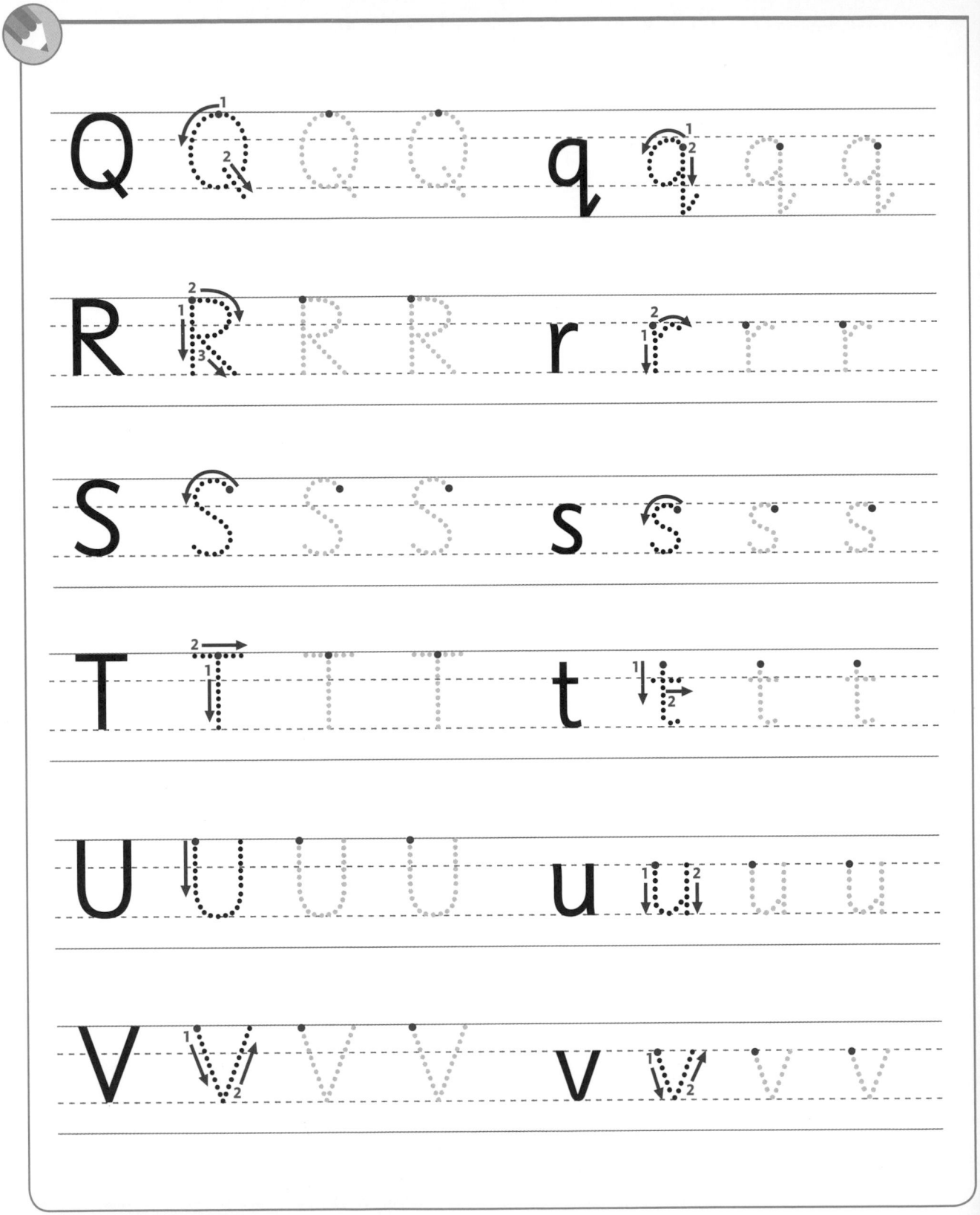
Q q
R r
S s
T t
U u
V v

W w
X x
Y y
Z z
Aa Bb Cc

Grammar guide

G1 To be

Use **to be** to talk about yourself and describe people and things.

Positive	Negative
I am/I'm	I'm not
You are/You're	You aren't
He is/He's	He isn't
She is/She's	She isn't
It is/It's	It isn't
We are/We're	We aren't
You are/You're	You aren't
They are/They're	They aren't

G2 Have

Use **have** to talk about things you own.

Positive	Negative
I have	I don't have
You have	You don't have
He has	He doesn't have
She has	She doesn't have
It has	It doesn't have
We have	We don't have
You have	You don't have
They have	They don't have

G3 Can

Use **can** to talk about things you are able to do.

Positive	Negative
I can	I can't
You can	You can't
He can	He can't
She can	She can't
It can	It can't
We can	We can't
You can	You can't
They can	They can't

G4 The present simple

Use the present simple to talk about opinions or things people do every day.

Positive	Negative
I like	I don't like
You like	You don't like
He likes	He doesn't like
She likes	She doesn't like
It likes	It doesn't like
We like	We don't like
You like	You don't like
They like	They don't like

G5 The present continuous

Use the present continuous to talk about things people are doing now.

Positive	Negative
I am walking/I'm walking	I'm not walking
You are walking/You're walking	You aren't walking
He is walking/He's walking	He isn't walking
She is walking/She's walking	She isn't walking
It is walking/It's walking	It isn't walking
We are walking/We're walking	We aren't walking
You are walking/You're walking	You aren't walking
They are walking/They're walking	They aren't walking

G6 Question words

Use question words such as **what**, **who**, **where**, and **when** to ask questions that can't be answered with **yes** or **no**.

Question word	Example question	Example answer
What	**What**'s that?	It's a crocodile.
Which	**Which** animal is big?	The dog is big.
Who	**Who**'s that?	It's Ben.
Whose	**Whose** camera is this?	It's mine.
When	**When** do you go to school?	I go to school in the morning.
Where	**Where**'s the cat?	It's under the table.
How	**How** old are you?	I'm nine years old.
How many	**How many** ducks are there?	There are five.
Why	**Why** do you like soccer?	It's fun!

G7 Irregular plurals

Most plurals are formed by adding an **s** or **es** to the end of a singular noun. However, some plurals are irregular and are spelled differently or don't change at all.

Singular	Plural
mouse	mice
tooth	teeth
foot	feet
child	children
woman	women
man	men
person	people
sheep	sheep
fish	fish

G8 Prepositions of place

Use prepositions of place to say where things are.

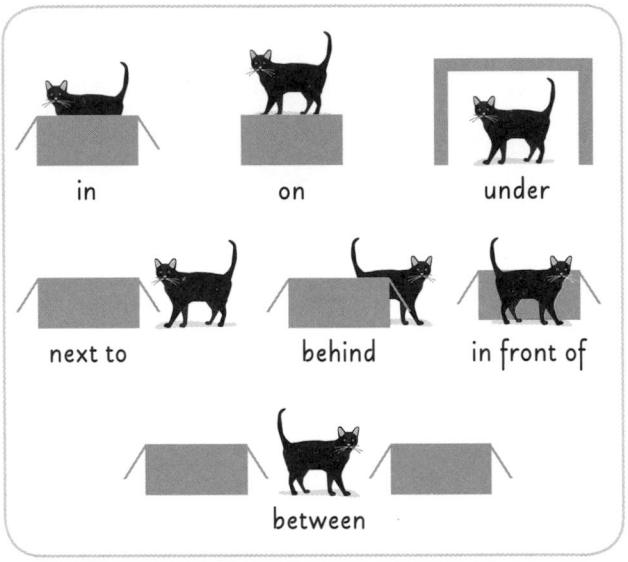

G9 This, that, these, those

Use **this**, **that**, **these**, and **those** to point things out.

	Singular	Plural
Near to you	This dog	These dogs
Far from you	That dog	Those dogs

G10 Pronouns, possessive adjectives, and possessive pronouns

Pronouns can replace nouns (names of people, places, and things) in a sentence.

Subject pronoun	Object pronoun	Possessive adjective	Possessive pronoun
Subject pronouns replace the person or thing that is doing an action. Example: Is **she** happy?	Object pronouns replace the person or thing that is having an action done to it. Example: I like **him**.	Possessive adjectives are used before a noun to say who something belongs to. Example: It's **my** book.	When you use a possessive pronoun, you don't need to use the noun. Example: It's **theirs**.
I	me	my	mine
you	you	your	yours
he	him	his	his
she	her	her	hers
it	it	its	its
we	us	our	ours
you	you	your	yours
they	them	their	theirs

G11 Conjunctions

Conjunctions, such as **and**, **but**, and **or**, are words that join two statements together.

Use **and** to join words in a positive statement.

I like oranges **and** bananas.

Use **but** to join a positive statement and a negative statement together.

I like oranges **but** I don't like bananas.

Use **or** to join words in a negative statement.

I don't like oranges **or** bananas.

G12 Common verbs

A verb is a word that describes an action.
This table shows some common English verbs.

Verb	Example sentence
give	Please **give** me that book.
hold	My baby brother can't **hold** a pen.
put	I **put** my toys in my toy box.
see	I can **see** an airplane in the sky!
stop	Where does this train **stop**?
talk	I **talk** to my friends at school.
tell	Can you **tell** me where the park is?
try	I **try** to speak English every day.

G13 Instructions

When you learn English or take a test, you might see these words in instructions.

Verbs

Nouns

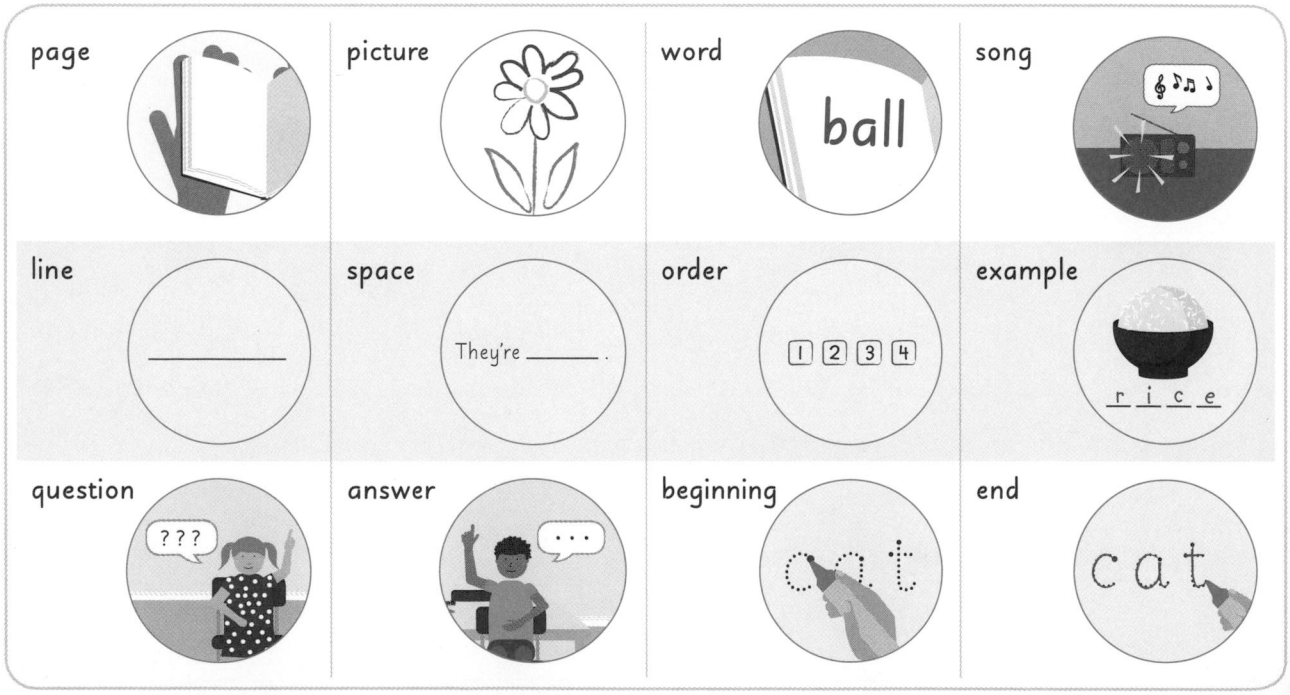

G14 Useful expressions

These expressions are useful for greeting people, saying goodbye, being polite, asking for information, or showing that you're happy.

Answers

1

1.3

1. Sofia
2. Max
3. Ben
4. Maria
5. Sara

1.6

1. eight
2. six
3. ten
4. nine
5. five

1.8

1. I'm **seven** years old.
2. I'm **six** years old.
3. I'm **10** years old.

2

2.2

1. classmate
2. book
3. teacher
4. board

2.4

1. listen
2. answer
3. sit down
4. add
5. pick up

2.5

1. stand up
2. show
3. tablet
4. alphabet
5. cupboard

2.7

1. What's **his** name?
2. **His** name's Hugo.
3. What's **her** name?

3

3.2

1. draw
2. read
3. count
4. spell

3.5

1. Let's count!
2. Let's write!
3. Let's read!
4. Let's draw!
5. Let's play!

3.6

1. Let's **count**!
2. Let's **write**!
3. Let's **read**!

3.8

1. fifteen
2. twenty
3. eighteen
4. thirteen

3.10

1 pens 2 teacher 3 chairs

4

4.2

six pencils

4.3

1 crayon 2 eraser 3 pencil
4 watch 5 pen

4.4

1 blue 2 brown 3 red
4 gray 5 purple

4.5

1 A 2 B 3 A 4 B

4.6

1 crayon 2 white 3 black
4 green 5 apple

4.8

1 It's an eraser.
2 It's an apple.
3 It's a watch.

4.10

1 They're **notepads**.
2 They're **rulers**.
3 They're **crayons**.
4 They're **erasers**.

4.13

1 purple 2 pink 3 orange
4 blue 5 green

4.14

1 It's yellow.
2 It's black.
3 It's purple.
4 It's red.

5

5.2

blue

5.3

1 monkey 2 tiger 3 hippo
4 whale 5 parrot

5.4

1 crocodile
2 bear
3 frog

5.5

1. lion
2. snake
3. lizard
4. penguin

5.6

1. B
2. A
3. A

5.9

1. It's a **giraffe**.
2. It's a **bear**.
3. It's a **crocodile**.

5.11

1. A
2. B
3. B
4. B
5. A

5.13

1. penguin
2. parrot
3. lizard
4. zebra
5. snake

6

6.2

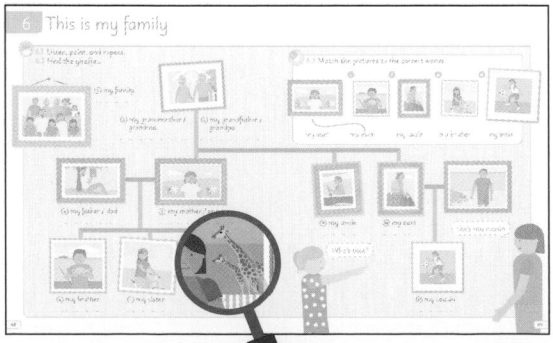

6.3

1. my brother
2. my aunt
3. my sister
4. my cousin

6.4

1. my dad
2. my mom
3. my sister
4. my brother

6.5

1. uncle
2. grandma
3. brother
4. mom
5. father

6.6

1. cousin
2. mother
3. sister
4. grandpa
5. aunt
6. dad

6.8

1. Who's this?
2. Who's this?
3. Who's that?

6.10

1. No, he isn't.
2. No, she isn't.
3. Yes, she is.

6.13

1. He's a vet.
2. She's a firefighter.
3. He's a farmer.
4. She's a doctor.
5. She's a police officer.

7

7.2

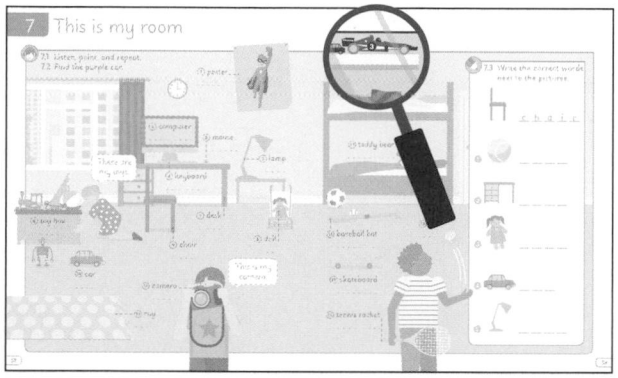

7.3

1. ball
2. desk
3. doll
4. car
5. lamp

7.4

1. teddy bear
2. camera
3. baseball bat
4. tennis racket

7.5

1. They're chairs.
2. They're dolls.
3. It's a skateboard.
4. It's a toy box.
5. It's a rug.

7.6

1. camera
2. poster
3. chair
4. car
5. lamp

7.8

1. These are my dolls.
2. These are my lamps.
3. This is my rug.

7.9

1. **That's** my poster.
2. **That's** my skateboard.
3. **Those are** my cars.

7.11

1. Max
2. Max
3. Sofia
4. Max
5. Sofia

7.13

1. Yes, I do.
2. Yes, I do.
3. No, I don't.

9

9.2

9.3

1. cold
2. sad
3. tired
4. happy

9.4

1. excited
2. hot
3. scared

9.5

1. sad
2. happy
3. cold
4. tired

9.6

1. hungry
2. happy
3. scared
4. sad
5. thirsty

9.9

1. B
2. A
3. A

9.10

1. They're happy.
2. We're hungry.
3. They're excited.

9.12

1. No, we aren't.
2. No, they aren't.
3. Yes, they are.

10

10.2

six fish

10.3

1. cat
2. tortoise
3. rabbit
4. dog

10.5

1. cat
2. mouse
3. dog

10.6

1. nice
2. young
3. big
4. beautiful
5. scary

10.7

c	r	m	a	n	d
o	y	o	u	n	g
l	s	u	v	e	g
l	c	s	e	r	c
a	y	e	t	d	a
r	a	b	b	i	t

10.10

1. tortoise
2. cat
3. dog
4. rabbit

10.11

1. Ben has a **mouse**.
2. She has a **dog**.
3. Sara has a **fish**.

10.13

1. No, she doesn't.
2. No, he doesn't.
3. Yes, he does.

10.14

1. A
2. B
3. B

10.16

1. Bonzo
2. Lee
3. Ted
4. Rex
5. Meg

11

11.2

Sara

11.3

1. head
2. mouth
3. hand
4. long hair

11.4

1. arm
2. toes
3. eye

11.5

1. fingers
2. hair
3. teeth
4. toes
5. mouth
6. ear

11.6

1. hair
2. nose
3. face
4. teeth
5. body

11.8

1. B
2. B
3. B
4. A
5. A

11.10

1. No, it doesn't.
2. Yes, it does.
3. Yes, it does.
4. No, it doesn't.

11.12

1. **Wave** your arms!
2. **Point** your finger!
3. **Move** your feet!

12

12.2

five cars

12.3

1. bus
2. truck
3. bike

12.4

1. school
2. hospital
3. park
4. helicopter
5. bike
6. train

12.5

1. bus
2. motorcycle
3. airplane
4. hospital

12.6

s	t	r	e	e	t
c	l	p	o	b	n
h	t	r	a	i	n
o	b	u	s	k	r
o	l	a	k	e	e
l	z	k	z	o	o

12.9

1. **There are** two trucks.
2. **There's** a school.
3. **There's** a zoo.
4. **There are** four cars.
5. **There are** three boats.

12.12

1. It's **next to** the store.
2. It's **in front of** the hospital.
3. It's **behind** the school.
4. It's **between** the park and the store.

12.14

1. A
2. B
3. A

13

13.2
the kitchen

13.3
1 kitchen 2 bathroom 3 bedroom

13.4
1 It's a bookcase. 2 It's a door.
3 It's a couch. 4 It's a television.
5 It's a refrigerator.

13.5
1 bookcase 2 table 3 flowers
4 clock 5 armchair 6 mat

13.6
1 hall 2 plants 3 window
4 lights 5 wall

13.9
1 B 2 A 3 B

13.12
1 No, there isn't. 2 Yes, there is.
3 Yes, there is. 4 No, there isn't.
5 No, there isn't.

13.14
1 No, there aren't. 2 Yes, there are.
3 Yes, there are. 4 No, there aren't.
5 Yes, there are.

15

15.2
11 sheep

15.3
1 bee 2 horse 3 barn
4 cow 5 goat

15.4
1 tail 2 tractor 3 barn
4 the sun 5 donkey

15.5
1 goat 2 horse
3 duck 4 tree

15.6
1 chicken 2 field 3 bee
4 pond 5 goat 6 tree

15.8
1 There are three. 2 There are four.
3 There's one.

15.10

1. They're in front of the barn.
2. They're under the tree.
3. They're in the field.
4. They're in the barn.
5. They're next to the pond.

15.13

This is my farm. My cow **is** under the tree. There 1 **are** four ducks 2 **in** the pond. The three chickens 3 **are** next to the horse. The donkey 4 **is** in the field, and five sheep 5 **are** in front of the barn.

16

16.2

16.3

1. ice hockey
2. tennis
3. basketball
4. badminton

16.4

1. table tennis
2. basketball
3. baseball

16.5

1. ice hockey
2. badminton
3. swimming
4. soccer

16.7

1. B
2. A
3. A
4. B
5. B

16.8

1. catch
2. swim
3. throw
4. kick
5. bounce

16.10

1. I **can** catch a ball.
2. I **can't** play ice hockey.
3. I **can** hit a ball.
4. I **can** swim.
5. I **can't** play table tennis.

16.12

1. Yes, **I can**.
2. **Can you** play baseball?
3. No, **I can't**.

16.14

1. Yes, she can.
2. No, she can't.
3. Yes, he can.

17

17.2

17.3

1. meat
2. onions
3. kiwis
4. lemons
5. pears

17.4

1. B
2. A
3. A
4. B

17.5

1. lime
2. orange
3. carrot
4. fish
5. coconut

17.6

1. yellow
2. brown
3. red
4. green
5. purple

17.9

1. I **don't like** watermelons.
2. I **like** apples.
3. I **like** lemons and limes.
4. I **don't like** carrots or onions.
5. I **don't like** tomatoes.

17.11

1. No, **I don't**.
2. Yes, **I do**.
3. Do you **like** mangoes?

17.13

1. May I have **a** banana, please?
2. May I have **an** orange, please?
3. May I have **some** vegetables, please?

18

18.2

8 stars

18.3

1. puppet
2. the moon
3. robot

18.4

1. board game
2. car
3. ball

18.5

1. robot
2. rocket
3. alien

18.6

1. It's a **monster**.
2. They're **stars**.
3. It's an **action figure**.

18.8

Sofia likes **cars**. Her cousin Eva doesn't like 1 **video games**. Ben likes 2 **rockets**, but his friend Sam doesn't like 3 **trains**.

18.9

1. Hugo **doesn't like** puppets.
2. Lucy **doesn't like** dolls.
3. Emma **likes** monsters.

18.11

1. No, she doesn't.
2. No, he doesn't.
3. Yes, she does.
4. Yes, he does.
5. No, she doesn't.

18.12

1. No, he doesn't.
2. Does she like dolls?
3. Yes, she does.

18.15

1. I don't.
2. Me too!
3. I don't.

19

19.2

19.3

1. dance
2. sing
3. draw pictures
4. take photos

19.4

1. B
2. A
3. A
4. B
5. A

19.5

1. sing
2. take photos
3. ride a bike
4. play the piano
5. paint

19.7

1. singing
2. drawing
3. reading
4. watching soccer

19.8

1. I enjoy taking photos.
2. I don't like riding a bike.
3. I like watching soccer.

19.10

1. Yes, I do.
2. No, I don't.
3. No, I don't.
4. Yes, I do.

21

21.2

blue

21.3

1. bag
2. jacket
3. hat

21.4

1. watch
2. dress
3. glasses
4. boot
5. baseball cap

21.5

1. B
2. A
3. A
4. B

21.6

1. It's a watch.
2. It's a jacket.
3. It's a sock.
4. It's a t-shirt.
5. It's a shoe.

21.9

1. B
2. A
3. A
4. B
5. B

21.11

1. No, I'm not.
2. Yes, I am.
3. Yes, I am.

21.13

1. **What** beautiful boots!
2. **What a** dirty sock!
3. **What** nice glasses!
4. **What a** nice shirt!
5. **What a** big purse!

22

22.2

three balls

22.3

1. drink juice
2. play soccer
3. throw a ball
4. listen to music
5. read a book

22.4

1. It's a shovel.
2. It's a shell.
3. It's a seagull.
4. It's a ship.
5. It's a bucket.

22.5

1. A 2. A 3. A 4. B 5. B

22.6

1. bucket 2. sand 3. run
4. shell 5. swim

22.8

1. She isn't swimming.
2. He isn't flying a kite.
3. She's drinking juice.

22.9

1. swimming
2. playing soccer
3. flying a kite
4. fishing

22.11

1. No, she isn't.
2. Yes, she is.
3. Yes, he is.

23

23.2

a burger

23.3

1. pie 2. salad 3. cake

23.4

1. orange 2. chocolate 3. juice
4. rice 5. salad

23.5

1. B 2. B 3. A

23.6

1. fries 2. fruit 3. sausages
4. burger 5. lemonade

23.8

1. fries 2. salad
3. noodles 4. orange

23.9

1. I'd like a drink, please.
2. I'd like some lemonade, please.
3. I'd like some fruit, please.

23.11

1. No, thank you.
2. Yes, please.
3. Yes, I would.

23.14

1. B 2. B 3. A 4. B 5. A

24

24.2

tennis

24.3

1. man
2. boy
3. men

24.4

1. people
2. boy
3. children
4. man
5. baby

24.5

p	e	r	s	o	n
e	c	h	i	l	d
o	s	i	g	e	b
p	b	k	i	d	o
l	y	r	r	d	y
e	o	h	l	i	h

24.6

1. woman 2. men 3. girl
4. women 5. kids

24.8

1. red bike
2. yellow bag
3. orange bike
4. green bike

24.9

1. The **girl's** ball is red.
2. The **baby's** doll is pink.
3. The **boy's** dog is dirty.
4. **Andy's** bike is yellow.
5. The **woman's** skirt is black.

24.12

1. It's theirs.
2. It's his.
3. It's hers.
4. It's ours.
5. It's yours.

25

25.2

Ben

25.3

1. I study English.
2. I eat lunch.
3. I get up.
4. I go to sleep.
5. I make my bed.

25.4

1. A
2. B
3. A
4. A
5. B

25.5

1. I get up.
2. I go to sleep.
3. I eat lunch.

25.6

1. I study English.
2. I eat lunch.
3. I walk to school.
4. I eat breakfast.
5. I brush my teeth.

25.8

1. It's six o'clock.
2. It's seven o'clock.
3. It's eleven o'clock.

25.10

1. I study English in the afternoon.
2. I phone my friend the evening.
3. I go to sleep at night.

25.12

1. I eat **breakfast**, and then I brush my teeth.
2. I **walk** to school at eight o'clock.
3. In the afternoon, **we** study English.
4. I eat dinner at **6 o'clock** with my family.
5. Then I **go to sleep** at seven o'clock.

25.14

1. eat
2. go
3. studies
4. gets
5. makes

25.17

1. I don't.
2. So do I.
3. I don't.

Grammar index

Each entry is followed by the number of the unit it appears in. Entries that appear in the **Grammar guide** have a **G** before them (for example, **G3**).

A
adjectives **2, 6, 9, 21, G10**
and **17, G11**
apostrophes **24**
articles **4, 5, 6, 17**

B
be (is/are) **1, 4, 5, 6, 9, 15, 21 21, 22, 25, G1**
but **G11**

C
can **16, G3**
common verbs **G12**
conjunctions **17, G11**
countable nouns **23**

D
do **17, 18**

G
greetings **1**

H
have **7, 10, 11, G2**
how? **1, G6**
how are you? **1**
how many? **15, G6**
how old are you? **1**

I
indefinite article **17**
instructions **G13**
irregular plurals **10, 11, 17, G7**

L
let's **3**
like+noun **17, 18**
like+verb+ing **19**

M, O
may **17**
me too **18**
mine **24**
one **10**
or **17, G11**

P
plurals **3, 10, 11, 17, G7**
possessive adjectives **1, 2, 6, G10**
possessive pronouns **24, G10**
prepositions **12, 13, 15, G8**
present continuous **21, 22, G5**
present simple **9, 17, 18, 25, G4**
pronouns **24, G10**

Q
question words **4, 5, 6, 10, 12, 15, 24, G6**

S
short forms **1**
singular and plural **3**
so do I **25**
some **17, 23**

T
telling the time **25**
that **5, 6, 7, 18, G9**
there is/there are **12, 13, 15**
these **4, 7, 25, G9**
this **4, 6, 7, 24, 25, G9**
those **5, 7, 18, G9**
to be *see be*
to have *see have*
to like *see like*

U
uncountable nouns **23**
useful expressions **G14**

W
what? **1, 2, 4, 5, G6**
what (a/an) **21**
when? **25, G6**
where? **12, G6**
which? **10, G6**
who? **6, G6**
whose? **24, G6**
why? **G6**
would like **23**

Word list

Each word is followed by the number of the unit it is taught in. Words that appear in the **Grammar guide** have a **G** before them (for example, **G3**).

KEY

adj	adjective
exp	expression
int	question word
n	noun
num	number
pl	plural
prep	preposition
pron	pronoun
v	verb

A

action figure *n* **18**
add *v* **2**
afternoon *n* **25**
airplane *n* **12**
airport *n* **12**
alien *n* **18**
alphabet *n* **2**
and *conj* **17, G11**
animal *n* **5**
answer *n* **G13**
answer *v* **2**
apartment block *n* **12**
apple *n* **4, 17**
arm *n* **11**
armchair *n* **13**
ask *v* **2**
at night *exp* **25**
aunt *n* **6**

B

baby (pl babies) *n* **24**
badminton *n* **16**
bag *n* **21, 24**
ball *n* **4, 7, 18, 22**
balloon *n* **18**
banana *n* **17**
barn *n* **15**
baseball *n* **16**
baseball bat *n* **7**
baseball cap *n* **21**
basketball *n* **16**
bathroom *n* **13**
bathtub *n* **13**
be (is/are) *v* **1, 4, 5, 6, 9, 15, 21, 22, 25, G1**
beach (pl beaches) *n* **22**
bean *n* **23**
bear *n* **5**
beautiful *adj* **10, 21**
bed *n* **7, 25**
bedroom *n* **13**
bee *n* **15**
beginning *n* **G13**
behind *prep* **12, G8**
between *prep* **12, G8**
big *adj* **10, 21**
bike *n* **12, 19**
bird *n* **5**
black *adj* **4**
blue *adj* **4**
board *n* **2**
board game *n* **18**
boat *n* **12**
body (pl bodies) *n* **11**
book *n* **2, 4, 22**
bookcase *n* **13**
bookstore *n* **12**
book pack *n* **4**
boot *n* **21**
bounce *v* **16**
boy *n* **24**
bread *n* **23**
breakfast *n* **23, 25**
brother *n* **6**
brown *adj* **4**
brush your teeth *v* **25**
bucket *n* **22**
burger *n* **23**
bus (pl buses) *n* **12**
but *conj* **G11**
bye *exp* **G14**

C

cake *n* **23**
call *v* **25**
camera *n* **7**
can *v* **16, G3**
car *n* **7, 12, 18**
carrot *n* **17**
cat *n* **10**
catch *v* **16**
chair *n* **2, 7, 13**
check off *v* **G13**
chef *n* **6**

chicken *n* **15, 23**
child (pl children) *n* **24**
children *n* **24**
chocolate *n* **23**
circle *v* **G13**
clap *v* **11**
classmate *n* **2**
classroom *n* **3**
clean *adj* **10, 21**
clock *n* **13, 25**
close *v* **2**
clothes *n* **21**
coconut *n* **17**
cold *adj* **9**
collar *n* **10**
color *n* **4**
color in *v* **G13**
computer *n* **7**
cool! *exp* **G14**
couch *n* **13**
count *v* **3, G13**
cousin *n* **6**
cow *n* **15**
crayon *n* **4**
crocodile *n* **5**
cross out *v* **G13**
cupboard *n* **2**

D

dad *n* **6**
dance *v* **19**
day *n* **25**
desk *n* **7**
dining room *n* **13**
dinner *n* **23, 25**
dirty *adj* **10, 21**
do you know? *exp* **G14**
do you want? *exp* **G14**
doctor *n* **6**
dog *n* **10**
doll *n* **7, 18**
donkey *n* **15**
don't worry *exp* **G14**
door *n* **13**
draw *v* **3**
dress (pl dresses) *n* **21**
drink *n* **23**
duck *n* **15**

E

ear *n* **11**
eat *v* **22, 23, 25**
egg *n* **23**
eight *num* **1**
eighteen *num* **3**
elephant *n* **5**
eleven *num* **3**
end *n* **G13**
enjoy *v* **19**
eraser *n* **4**
evening *n* **25**
example *n* **G13**
excited *adj* **9**
excuse me *exp* **G14**
eye *n* **11**

F

face *n* **11**
fair *n* **9**
family (pl families) *n* **6**
fantastic! *exp* **G14**
farm *n* **15**
farmer *n* **6**
father *n* **6**
favorite *adj* **5**
feet *n* **11**
field *n* **15**
fifteen *num* **3**
find *v* **2**
fine *adj* **1**
finger *n* **11**
fire station *n* **12**
firefighter *n* **6**
fish (pl fish) *n* **10, 17, 23**
fish *v* **22**
five *num* **1**
floor *n* **13**
flower *n* **13**
fly a kite *v* **22**
food market *n* **17**
foot (pl feet) *n* **11**
four *num* **1**
fourteen *num* **3**
Friday *n* **25**
friend *n* **1, 25**
fries *n* **23**
frog *n* **5**
fruit *n* **17, 23**

G

game *n* **18**
garden *n* **13**
get up *v* **25**
giraffe *n* **5**

girl *n* **24**
give *v* **G12**
glasses *n* **21**
go home *v* **25**
go swimming *v* **25**
go to sleep *v* **25**
goat *n* **15**
good morning *exp* **G14**
goodbye *exp* **G14**
grandfather/grandpa *n* **6**
grandmother/grandma *n* **6**
grape *n* **17**
green *adj* **4**
gray *adj* **4**
guitar *n* **19**

H

hair *n* **11**
hall *n* **13**
hand *n* **11**
happy *adj* **9**
hat *n* **21**
have *v* **7, 10, 11, 17, G2**
he *pron* **6**
head *n* **11**
helicopter *n* **12**
hello *exp* **1, G14**
her *adj* **2, G10**
hers *pron* **24**
hi *exp* **1**
hippo *n* **5**
his *adj* **2, G10**
his *pron* **24**
hit *v* **16**
hobby (pl hobbies) *n* **19**
hold *v* **G12**
home *n* **13, 25**
hooray! *exp* **G14**
horse *n* **15**
hospital *n* **12**
hot *adj* **9**
house *n* **12**
how? *int* **1, G6**
how many? *int* **15, G6**
hungry *adj* **9**

I, J, K

ice cream *n* **22**
ice hockey *n* **16**
I'm sorry *exp* **G14**
in *prep* **13, 15, G8**
in front of *prep* **12, G8**
in the afternoon *exp* **25**
in the evening *exp* **25**
in the morning *exp* **25**
jacket *n* **21**
jeans *n* **21**
jellyfish (pl jellyfish) *n* **22**
juice *n* **22, 23**
jump *v* **16**
keyboard *n* **7**
kick *v* **16**
kid *n* **24**
kitchen *n* **13**
kite *n* **22**
kiwi *n* **17**

L

lake *n* **12**
lamp *n* **7**
leg *n* **11**
lemon *n* **17**
lemonade *n* **23**
letter *n* **2**
light *n* **13**
like *v* **17, 18, 19, 23**
lime *n* **17**
line *n* **G13**
lion *n* **5**
listen *v* **2, G13**
listen to music *v* **22**
live *v* **12**
living room *n* **13**
lizard *n* **5**
long *adj* **11**
look (at) *v* **2, G13**
love *v* **18, G14**
lunch *n* **23, 25**
lunchtime *n* **23**

M

make my bed *v* **25**
man (pl men) *n* **24**
mango (pl mangoes) *n* **17**
mat *n* **13**
match *v* **G13**
may *v* **17**
me *pron* **6**
meat *n* **17**
meatball *n* **23**
men *n* **24**
milk *n* **23**

mine *pron* **24**
mirror *n* **13**
mom *n* **6**
Monday *n* **25**
monkey *n* **5**
monster *n* **18**
moon, the *n* **18**
morning *n* **25**
mother *n* **6**
motorcycle *n* **12**
mouse (pl mice) *n* **7, 10**
mouth *n* **11**
move *v* **11**
music *n* **22**
my *adj* **1, 4, 5, 6, 7, 11, 13, 21, 25, G10**

N

name *n* **1, 2**
next to *prep* **12, G8**
nice *adj* **10, 21**
night *n* **25**
nine *num* **1**
nineteen *num* **3**
no, thank you *exp* **23**
noodles *n* **23**
nose *n* **11**
notepad *n* **4**
number *n* **2**

O

o'clock *adv* **25, G14**
ocean *n* **22**
oh dear *exp* **G14**
old *adj* **10**
on *prep* **13, G8**
one *num* **1**
one *pron* **10**
onion *n* **17**
open *v* **2**
or *conj* **17, G11**
orange *adj* **4**
orange *n* **17, 23**
order *n* **G13**
our *adj* **G10**
ours *pron* **24**

P

page *n* **G13**
paint *v* **3, 19**
pants *n* **21**
paper *n* **4**
pardon? *int* **G14**
park *n* **12, 24**
parrot *n* **5**
party (pl parties) *n* **21**
pasta *n* **23**
pea *n* **23**
pear *n* **17**
pen *n* **2, 4**
pencil *n* **2, 4**
penguin *n* **5**
people *n* **24**
person (pl people) *n* **24**
pet *n* **10**
photo *n* **19**
piano *n* **19**
pick up *v* **2**
picture *n* **19, G13**
pie *n* **23**
pig *n* **15**
pineapple *n* **17**
pink *adj* **4**
plant *n* **13**
play *v* **3, 16**
play a musical instrument *v* **19**
play a sport *v* **16**
playground *n* **2**
please *adv* **17, 23, G14**
point *v* **11, G13**
polar bear *n* **5**
police officer *n* **6**
pond *n* **15**
poster *n* **7**
potato (pl potatoes) *n* **17, 23**
puppet *n* **18**
purple *adj* **4**
purse *n* **21**
put *v* **G12**

Q

question *n* **G13**

R

rabbit *n* **10**
read *v* **3, 19, G13**
really *adv* **9**
red *adj* **4**
refrigerator *n* **13**
repeat *v* **G13**
rice *n* **23**
ride a bike *v* **19**

robot *n* **11, 18**
rocket *n* **18**
room *n* **7, 13**
rug *n* **7**
ruler *n* **4**
run *v* **16, 22**

S

sad *adj* **9**
salad *n* **23**
sand *n* **22**
Saturday *n* **25**
sausage *n* **23**
scared *adj* **9**
scary *adj* **10**
school *n* **2, 12, 25**
seagull *n* **22**
see *v* **G12**
see you! *exp* **G14**
seven *num* **1**
seventeen *num* **3**
she *pron* **6**
sheep (pl sheep) *n* **15**
shell *n* **22**
ship *n* **22**
shirt *n* **21**
shoe *n* **21**
short hair *n* **11**
shorts *n* **21**
shovel *n* **22**
show *v* **2**
sing *v* **19**
sister *n* **6**
sit down *v* **2**
six *num* **1**
sixteen *num* **3**
skateboard *n* **7**
skateboard *v* **19**
skirt *n* **21**
sleep, go to *v* **25**
small *adj* **10**
snake *n* **5**
soccer *n* **16, 19, 22**
sock *n* **21**
song *n* **G13**
sorry, I'm *exp* **G14**
space *n* **G13**
spell *v* **3**
spider *n* **10**
sport *n* **16**
stand up *v* **2**
star *n* **18**
stop *v* **G12**
street *n* **12**
store *n* **12**
study *v* **25**
study English *v* **25**
sun, the *n* **15**
Sunday *n* **25**
surf *v* **22**
sweet *n* **23**
swim *v* **16, 22**
swimming *n* **16**

T

table *n* **13**
table tennis *n* **16**
tablet *n* **2**
tail *n* **15**
take photos *v* **19**
talk *v* **G12**
teacher *n* **2, 6**
teddy bear *n* **7, 18**
teeth *n* **11, 25**
television/TV *n* **13**
tell *v* **G12**
ten *num* **1**
tennis *n* **16**
tennis racket *n* **7**
thank you/thanks *exp* **1, 23**
that *pron* **5, 6, 7, 18, G9**
their *adj* **G10**
the moon *n* **18**
the sun *n* **15**
theirs *pron* **23**
these *pron* **4, 7, 25, G9**
thing *n* **4**
thirsty *adj* **9**
thirteen *num* **3**
this *pron* **4, 6, 7, G9**
those *pron* **5, 7, G9**
three *num* **1**
throw *v* **16, 22**
Thursday *n* **25**
tiger *n* **5**
time *n* **25**
tired *adj* **9**
toe *n* **11**
tomato (pl tomatoes) *n* **17**
tooth (pl teeth) *n* **11**
tortoise *n* **10**
touch *v* **11**
town *n* **12**
toy *n* **7**
toy box (pl toy boxes) *n* **7**
toy store *n* **18**

tractor *n* **15**
train *n* **12, 18**
tree *n* **15**
truck *n* **12**
try *v* **G12**
t-shirt *n* **21**
Tuesday *n* **25**
TV *n* **13**
twelve *num* **3**
twenty *num* **3**
two *num* **1**

U

uncle *n* **6**
under *prep* **13, 15, G8**

V

vegetable *n* **17**
very *adv* **9**
vet *n* **6, 10**
video game *n* **18**

W

wake up *v* **25**
walk *v* **25**
walk to school *v* **25**
wall *n* **13**
want *v* **G14**
watch (pl watches) *n* **4, 21**
watch soccer *v* **19**
water *n* **23**
watermelon *n* **17**
wave *v* **11**
wear *v* **21**
Wednesday *n* **25**
whale *n* **5**
what? *int* **1, 2, 4, 5, G6**
what time? *int* **25, G14**
when? *int* **25, G6**
where? *int* **12, G6**
which? *int* **10, G6**
white *adj* **4**
who? *int* **6, G6**
whose? *int* **24, G6**
why? *int* **G6**
window *n* **13**
woman (pl women) *n* **24**
women *n* **24**
word *n* **G13**
worry, don't *exp* **G14**
would *v* **23**
write *v* **3, G13**

Y

year *n* **1**
yellow *adj* **4**
yes, please *exp* **23, G14**
young *adj* **10**
your *adj* **5, 6, G10**
yours *pron* **24**

Z

zebra *n* **5**
zoo *n* **12**

Acknowledgments

The publisher would like to thank:

Rishi Bryan and Soma B. Chowdhury for editorial assistance; Gus Scott, Francis Wong, and Steve Woosnam-Savage for design and illustration assistance; Sourabh Challariya, Chhaya Sajwan, and Arunesh Talapatra for design assistance; Kayla Dugger, Lori Hand, and Steph Noviss for proofreading; Tim Woolf for songwriting; Christine Stroyan and Lizzie Davey for audio recording management; Susan Millership for audio script management; and ID Audio for audio recording and production.

All images are copyright DK. For more information, please visit **www.dkimages.com.**